Unshakeable LeadHERship

Redefining Power Through

Connection & Purpose

Featuring **Linda Fisk**, LeadHERship Global

Published by **Michael Beas,** Atlas Elite Publishing Partners

Unshakeable LeadHERship
An Anthology Featuring Linda Fisk, LeadHERship Global
Published by Michael Beas, Atlas Elite Publishing Partners

ATLAS ELITE
PUBLISHING

https://atlaselitepublishingpartners.com

eBook ISBN: 978-1-962825-92-4
Paperback ISBN: 978-1-962825-93-1

Table of contents

Foreword

Leadership at the highest level is not defined by authority or position, it is defined by influence, trust, and the ability to move people toward a shared vision. True leadership is measured not by what we control, but by what we empower.

Long before I built companies, advised executives, or worked alongside global leaders, I learned the foundations of leadership from the women who shaped my worldview, beginning with my mother, **Martha Espigul**.

She was a formidable executive in an era when women were rarely welcomed into senior sales roles, let alone respected within them. As one of the first female sales executives in a male-dominated Fortune 500 company, she navigated resistance with intelligence, resilience, and results. She didn't lead through force, she led through credibility. She didn't demand influence, she earned it.

From her, I learned that leadership is not performative. It is principled. It is consistent. And it is built on relationships.

That foundation was strengthened throughout my career by extraordinary women leaders who each shaped how I define leadership today.

During my time at Liberty Mutual, **Margarita Kovacs** taught me the discipline of sales excellence and management. She instilled in me the understanding that preparation creates confidence, clarity drives performance, and accountability is a form of respect, for clients, teams, and oneself.

Later, **Tricia Benn**, CEO of C-Suite Network, reinforced the strategic power of community. She demonstrated that leadership does not scale in isolation, that when leaders are intentionally connected, supported, and aligned, organizations grow stronger and impact multiplies. Community, when built with purpose, becomes a competitive advantage.

Through **Linda Fisk**, Founder of LeadHERship Global, I came to understand that connection is not a soft skill; it is a leadership imperative. She exemplifies the truth that trust, inclusion, and human connection are not just values; they are the infrastructure of sustainable leadership. In a world driven by metrics and momentum, she reminds us that relationships remain the most valuable currency we possess.

Leadership, however, is not only shaped by mentors, but it is also shaped by those we choose to trust and empower.

I am proud to lead alongside my daughter, **Schiammarelly Pinckert Nieme**, whom I have entrusted as President of Atlas Elite Publishing Partners. Her leadership reflects the next generation of empowered executives, principled, decisive, values-driven, and unafraid to lead with both strength and empathy. Watching her step confidently into leadership reinforces my belief that the future of business is in capable, connected hands.

I am equally grateful for **Dar Dowling**, Film Producer, Artist, Author, and Executive Vice President of Atlas Elite Publishing Partners. Her creative vision, executive leadership, and unwavering integrity elevate everything she touches, reminding us that leadership thrives at the intersection of strategy and storytelling.

And above all, I am fortunate to share my life with my wife, **Kristine Kennedy**, a remarkable business executive in her own right. She has taught me the power of organization, discipline, and operational clarity, proof that sustainable leadership is built not only on vision, but on structure and execution.

I am proud to be surrounded, professionally and personally, by so many empowered female leaders. Their influence is woven into the fabric of who I am as a leader and reflected throughout *Unshakeable LeadHERship: Redefining Power Through Connection & Purpose*.

This book is not about leading louder or faster. It is about leading better. It is about aligning vision with purpose, strategy with humanity, and ambition with responsibility. The leaders featured in these pages demonstrate that when women lead with authenticity, connection, and conviction, organizations and societies are stronger for it.

Where vision becomes action. Where women lead with impact.

For executives navigating complexity, founders scaling purpose-driven organizations, and leaders committed to shaping the future, this book serves as both a compass and a catalyst. It challenges outdated models of power and offers a more enduring blueprint, one rooted in trust, collaboration, and unshakeable clarity.

The future of leadership belongs to those who understand that connection fuels performance, purpose drives resilience, and influence is built through integrity.

It is an honor to introduce **_Unshakeable LeadHERship: Redefining Power Through Connection & Purpose._** May it inspire you to lead with intention, invest in connection, and redefine what powerful leadership truly looks like.

Michael Beas -

CEO, Atlas Elite Publishing Partners, a Beas Group Company.

Amy Vasterling

Inner Knowing and Collective Transformation

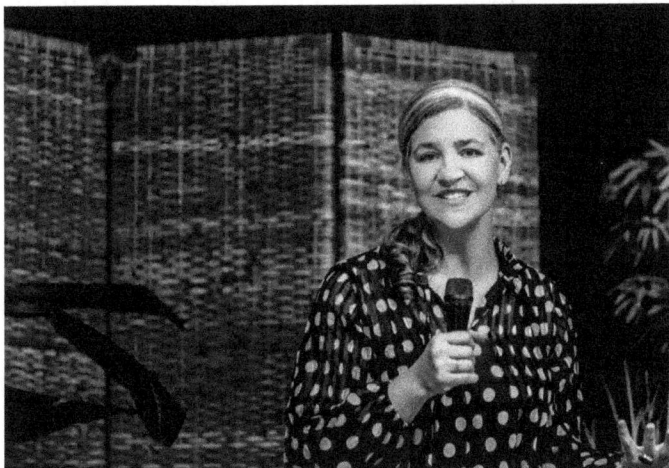

Amy Cerny Vasterling offers a transformative—and refreshingly quiet—alternative: Know. Her upcoming book, Know: Where the Status Quo Ends and You Come to Life (releasing September 16, 2025), blends memoir, manifesto, and intuitive field guide into a single, potent invitation: to step out of "The Model," a silent societal script that defines worth through hierarchy, and into the innate wisdom of what she calls "Personal Knowing."

At the core of Vasterling's work is her bold concept of "collapsing narcissism," a term drawn from 22 years of observational research.

Through this lens, she examines how control-based structures—rooted in childhood misattunements—strip individuals of their self-governance. "As babies, we know when we're hungry, tired, or upset," Vasterling explains. "But when our caregivers dismiss or mislabel these cues, we begin to doubt ourselves. We stop asking for what we need." That fracture, she argues, grows into a lifetime of posturing, striving, and self-abandonment—what she calls "acting inside The Model."

Her findings suggest that societal narcissism—evidenced in power imbalances, immaturity in leadership, and a general emotional stunting—stems from this early disconnect.

"We've not matured collectively past age 16 emotionally," she says. "That's how deeply embedded the hierarchy and control patterns have become." But it's not all bleak: Vasterling insists that reclaiming our internal compass through Personal Knowing is the way forward. This grounded self-awareness allows us to ask, "Is this for me?" and act from alignment rather than reaction.

A central figure in this paradigm shift? Highly Sensitive Persons (HSPs). Vasterling, an HSP herself, sees them as society's early-warning system—like elephants that sense natural disasters before they strike. "HSPs process more, see patterns faster, and want deeply to help," she explains. Yet many are trapped in a feedback loop of permission-seeking and self-doubt. Her message to them is clear: You are the signalers. Your discomfort is a signpost that the system must change—and you're here to guide that change.

This ethos pulses through Know. Far from a conventional self-help manual, the book is a clarion call for those who feel anxious, stuck, or disconnected—not as a personal failing, but as evidence of living inside The Model. "The Model," she says, "is upheld by control masquerading as power. But true power is knowing. It's quiet. It's calm. And it's deeply personal." Writing the book was no small feat; it took Vasterling five years, three of them working with an editor. "We think fast is better, but truth takes time," she reflects. "There was a calm in me as I wrote, a knowing that this was meant to come through."

The process wasn't just creative—it was transformative. As she moved deeper into the work, Vasterling realized that the outcome was more than personal—it was social. "Two years in, I saw the result was natural equality," she recalls. "I cried. After a lifetime in spaces that prioritized disconnection, this felt like real hope."

Natural equality, as she defines it, is not about sameness. It's about each person being fully themselves, unencumbered by imposed roles or outdated structures. It's the opposite of hierarchy—and the antithesis of narcissism.

So how do we begin to break free from The Model in practice? Vasterling's method is what she calls "Snoopy Simple." The phrase is playful, but the approach is profound: begin with what's easy, with what feels right.

"It's logical to agree that it's easiest to be who you truly are," she says. "But The Model convinces us to stay in jobs, relationships, and roles that drain us."

She illustrates this with a story from her high school ski team. After a teammate dramatically improved her race time, the coach praised her not by comparing her to others, but by affirming what she herself had accomplished. The result? Every team member improved at the next race. "That's inversion," Vasterling says. "We heal what broke us—by seeing and naming what's already working in each person."

This spirit of affirmation and gentle transformation also informs her Wisdom Gatherings—monthly community events for women, creatives, and HSPs. Equal parts energy reading, support circle, and intuitive coaching, these gatherings provide the repetition needed to shift lifelong patterns. "It's like learning a new language," she explains. "The gatherings give us a place to talk about it, to be seen, and to realize we're not alone."

For Vasterling, community is key to dismantling The Model. "When we find people who meet us in a Model-free way—even if just for now—we begin to remember who we are. That's where the real change begins."

Ultimately, Know is not a guidebook for perfection. It's a permission slip to be human—fully, expressively, and imperfectly so. "We didn't create The Model, but it is ours to heal," Vasterling says. "And when we do, we rediscover what it means to be alive—not just surviving, but truly, deeply living."

Christine Williams

Building Profit with Purpose

In a business world often dominated by hustle culture, quick wins, and aggressive marketing, Christine Williams is rewriting the rules. Her new book, *The Soulful Abundance System®*, offers a fresh, heart-centered roadmap for wellness coaches, healers, and entrepreneurs who are ready to scale their businesses without sacrificing integrity, authenticity, or joy.

Williams' approach is grounded in lived experience. Before becoming a business mentor, she was a certified wellness practitioner who found herself struggling to attract clients despite a deep passion for helping others. "The health and wellness certifications did not teach how to actually attract clients and sell my programs," she explains.

"The only tactic I was taught was to book a discovery session and give a free coaching to sell my program. This felt like a bait and switch to me and out of alignment with how I would have wanted to be treated."

That moment of misalignment became her turning point. Williams began questioning the transactional nature of traditional sales methods and started developing a more relationship-driven approach—one rooted in trust, service, and genuine connection. "I quickly realized that without the nurturing required to build trust and safety with a potential client, cold leads don't buy," she says.

"So I created a method to serve first, develop trust and safety, and lead with value *before* inviting someone into a conversation to explore working with me."

That philosophy evolved into *The Soulful Abundance System*®—a six-step framework that has since guided countless entrepreneurs from survival mode to greater stability and abundance. The process integrates both strategy and spirituality, moving practitioners beyond burnout and into balance.

One of the most talked-about elements of Williams' framework is "Sacred Visibility," a concept that turns the high-pressure idea of omnipresence on its head. Instead of chasing algorithms or posting endlessly, Williams teaches her clients to show up with focus and intention. "Creating Sacred Visibility is not about being on in all the places or platforms," she says. "It's about picking the ones where your ideal client spends the most amount of time. Burnout happens when there is lack of clarity on where your ideal client is. We simplify this process to focus on one social media platform and one email list before adding anything else."

That philosophy of simplicity and soul extends to the financial side of business as well. One of the myths Williams is determined to dismantle is the notion that wellness practitioners shouldn't charge for their services. "So many wellness coaches and entrepreneurs have a hard time charging because they want to help people," she explains. "But what they don't realize is that when clients invest, that commitment becomes part of their accountability. It gives them skin in the game and helps them actually get results."

For Williams, charging for your work isn't about greed—it's about honoring the value of transformation. "There's a difference between being a philanthropist and a business owner," she says. "If you want to be a philanthropist, you need to have a profitable business first. A business needs paying clients."

At the heart of her book lies another key principle: "Heart-Led Sales." Williams contrasts this with traditional sales strategies that prioritize conversion over connection. "Heart-Led Sales is completely different from the traditional model of trying to convert cold leads," she says. "We serve first, give value, and build a relationship before inviting someone into a consultation.

When this happens, there's no need to convince or overcome objections—they're already handled naturally through trust."

This approach reframes selling as an act of service rather than persuasion. It's about guiding potential clients toward empowered decisions, not pushing them into commitments. "It feels so much better for both parties," Williams adds. "The energy is clean and supportive instead of desperate or salesy."

While *The Soulful Abundance System*® is structured around six stages—Clarity, Align, Nurture, Invite, Serve, and Scale—Williams insists that breakthroughs are deeply personal. "The breakthrough is individual to the client depending on where their struggle is," she says. "Some experience transformation in the Align stage, stepping into the identity of an empowered business owner. Others have their moment when they realize that sales don't require aggressive tactics, or when they finally design a freedom schedule that serves their life and business."

Perhaps the most comforting message of the book is its reminder that scaling doesn't have to mean losing touch with one's soul. Williams redefines growth not as "doing more" but as "aligning better." "Scaling doesn't mean working harder or more hours," she emphasizes. "It means leveraging your time and getting clear on a business model that fits the way you want to serve."

For some, that might mean shifting from one-on-one sessions to group programs, or automating systems that free up mental space. "The key is deciding first what your energetic capacity is and then creating a business model to support that," Williams says. "You get to decide how big or small your business should be."

In an age where many entrepreneurs feel torn between purpose and profit, Christine Williams offers a refreshing middle path—one where business becomes an act of service, selling becomes soulful, and success feels aligned. Her message is simple yet profound: abundance doesn't come from doing more—it comes from doing what's right for your soul.

The Soulful Abundance System® is more than a book; it's a movement toward building businesses that thrive not only in numbers but in heart, purpose, and integrity. And in a world desperate for authenticity, that might be the most revolutionary system of all.

Debbie Harris

Why "Dieting Sucks" for Women Over 40

For many women, midlife can feel like a betrayal. After decades of dieting, exercising, and trying various weight-loss plans, the scale refuses to budge. Menopause brings its own set of challenges: weight gain, disrupted sleep, mood swings, and hormonal upheaval. It's no wonder women over 40 might feel exhausted, frustrated, and sometimes defeated by solutions that simply weren't designed for them.

That's precisely the problem that Debbie Harris, certified Integrative Nutrition Health Coach and Certified Hypnotist, addresses in her book, *Dieting Sucks for Women Over 40: 30 to Life – The Ultimate Weight Loss and Hormone Balancing Solution.*

Harris knows firsthand the struggle of decades spent cycling through diets with little lasting success, and she offers a potentially different approach, grounded in biology, psychology, and compassion.

Why Traditional Dieting Fails

"Most diets were never designed for women like us," Harris says openly. "They tend to overlook the hormonal changes that start creeping in during perimenopause and menopause: our stress levels, sleep patterns, metabolism, everything shifts." Women who were able to lose weight in their 20s and 30s often hit an invisible wall in midlife. Hot flashes, night sweats, mood changes, and stubborn belly fat can become a consistent frustration. Add a lifetime of dieting, feelings of shame, and hours spent at the gym with limited results, and the emotional toll can be hard to bear.

Harris points out a lesser-known culprit: cortisol, the stress hormone. "Many women are unaware that they may be inadvertently raising their cortisol levels by exercising in ways that aren't productive," she explains.

Elevated cortisol may exacerbate weight gain, particularly around the abdomen, and contribute to fatigue, irritability, and sleep disturbances. Without guidance on how to exercise and eat in alignment with their changing bodies, women might spiral into burnout instead of finding balance.

Biological and Emotional Shifts

Menopause doesn't just bring physical changes; it's also a deeply emotional season of life. "Cortisol goes haywire, insulin sensitivity changes, estrogen levels decrease, and we lose muscle faster," Harris explains.

These shifts can make weight loss seem nearly impossible. Emotionally, women face identity changes, shifts in libido, work pressures, caregiving demands, and often a sense of invisibility. Self-care falls to the bottom of the list, and food might become both a comfort and a battleground.

Harris' own experience reflects this reality. "I used to feel like I was losing my mind," she recalls, "that I would go crazy on someone who cut me off in traffic." Mood swings, she notes, are not trivial; they can interact with every other physical and emotional change, making traditional diet advice feel futile and unfair.

Shame and Internalized Failure

One of the most destructive forces Harris identifies is shame. Decades of dieting, comparison to media ideals, and feeling uncomfortable in one's own body can create a powerful sense of failure.

"We feel powerless, out of control," she says. "Many women tell me, 'I have failed so many times, I am afraid to try again.' This is something that profoundly affects me. I want them to know that I have taken that journey and there is a way out of the darkness."

She emphasizes that food is lifelong, and unlike other habits or addictions, it cannot be avoided entirely. "So much is built into our relationship with food," she explains. "It is with us our whole life, and you cannot go 'cold turkey' with food the way you can sometimes do with other addictions."

Redefining Success in Midlife

Harris encourages women to rethink what success truly means. It's not measured by a number on a scale or fitting into a certain size. Instead, success is about balance, energy, and freedom. "Success is waking up with energy, sleeping well, walking with ease, and fitting into your life," she says. "It's releasing the emotional weight, not just the pounds. And it's eating sushi or birthday cake without spiraling into guilt. That's real success. It's knowing that you are in control, not food."

It's Never Too Late to Transform Your Relationship with Food

Perhaps the most empowering aspect of Harris' message is that transformation is possible at any age. She began her own journey in her early 60s, after decades of dieting and frustration. Today, she coaches women in their 50s, 60s, and even 70s, helping them balance hormones, regain energy, and cultivate a positive, guilt-free relationship with food.

"It's never too late," she believes. "I have worked with women in their 70s who finally understood their relationship with food, balanced their bodies, and are enjoying life without guilt over what they eat or don't eat. It's freedom, and you may achieve it at any age."

A Revolutionary Approach

Harris' book is not a fad diet or restrictive plan. Instead, it offers a comprehensive framework for women over 40, combining hormone-smart nutrition, mindset shifts, and practical strategies that respect the realities of midlife bodies. Her approach incorporates self-hypnosis, journaling, and personalized guidance, helping women identify emotional triggers, reduce stress, and develop sustainable habits that can last.

For Harris, the mission is as much about empowerment as it is about weight loss. "I want women to know that the struggle isn't their fault," she says. "They've just never been given the right tools. Midlife isn't a dead end, it's an invitation to change the story, break the cycle, and come home to their bodies with love, clarity, and confidence."

The Takeaway

Dieting Sucks for Women Over 40: 30 to Life is more than a book; it's a guide to freedom. Freedom from shame, restriction, and unrealistic expectations. Freedom to enjoy food, feel strong, and honor the changes that come with midlife. With warmth, expertise, and compassion, Debbie Harris shows women that midlife can be a season of growth, vitality, and empowerment.

Debra L. Morrison

Grief, Growth, and Financial Clarity

When a woman loses her husband, she loses more than a life partner — she often loses her sense of security, direction, and identity. In *My Husband Died, Now What?: A Widow's Guide to Grief Recovery & Smart Financial Decisions*, CERTIFIED FINANCIAL PLANNER(™) and Certified Grief Coach and widowhood advocate Debra L. Morrison offers widows a compassionate, practical blueprint to navigate both the emotional and financial storms that follow such a profound loss.

Morrison's book stands out by combining heartfelt empathy with professional expertise.

Rather than offering only sympathy, she delivers an actionable roadmap that widows can follow to regain agency over their lives, both emotionally and financially.

A Broader, More Realistic View of Grief

Morrison expands the common understanding of grief beyond the usual notion of sadness and mourning. She defines grief as "the overarching process of reacting to any significant loss," and emphasizes that it's a highly personal, evolving journey.

"People experience grief in many different ways," Morrison explains. "There is no single correct path or timeline. Grieving is often nonlinear, and it's vital for widows to feel free to express their stories without judgment."

This focus on storytelling and personal expression is critical, as Morrison highlights the need to shed societal expectations about how one "should" grieve. She gently reminds readers and their support networks that "withholding judgment and letting go of wishing for a different yesterday" are key steps toward healing.

Challenging Common Grief Myths

One of the most harmful myths Morrison tackles head-on is the belief that "time heals all wounds." She calls this idea "as insane as imagining a broken bone will heal without proper treatment." Instead, she underscores that grief requires active, intentional participation. Widows benefit from strategic tools, support networks, and steps designed to help them move forward, not away from their pain, but through it.

Morrison also challenges the pressure widows often feel to "stay strong" or move quickly through grief. She encourages allowing grace for confusion, forgetfulness, and emotional ups and downs, emphasizing that it's not only okay to change your mind or feelings suddenly, but vital to do so without self-judgment.

When Grief and Finances Collide

What makes *My Husband Died, Now What?* especially unique and invaluable is its frank discussion about money — a topic many grief guides sidestep. As a CERTIFIED FINANCIAL PLANNERr™, Morrison intimately understands the double bind widows face: emotional devastation paired with looming financial decisions.

Morrison explains that while many try to separate emotions from intellect when managing finances, in reality they are "deeply interwoven."

She draws from research in Neuro-Linguistic Programming that shows when emotions run high, intellectual clarity diminishes and vice versa. This insight leads her to recommend that widows initially focus on emoting fully before engaging their intellect to tackle complicated financial decisions.

"Financial clarity comes with time," Morrison writes. "As widows' values become clearer, they can align their financial lives with new goals, ideally with the guidance of a fiduciary CERTIFIED FINANCIAL PLANNER(™) who acts in their best interests."

Redefining Urgency: Why Most Decisions Can Wait

Widows frequently feel pressured to act quickly selling homes, changing investments, rewriting wills. Morrison warns that these hurried actions often cause regret. "There's an understandable urge to 'do something,' but acting in the throes of grief is a recipe for costly tax and investment mistakes," she cautions.

Instead, she advocates for patience and self-compassion, encouraging widows to grant themselves the time needed to regain perspective before making major financial decisions.

The Healing Power of Community and Support

Morrison stresses that community support plays a vital role in widowhood recovery, though it's often misunderstood or lacking. "Widows need people to check in on them—but they also need space and control over their social interactions," she notes.

One touching recommendation is the use of simple signals, like tying a green handkerchief to a door handle, to indicate the widow is open to visitors or a red handkerchief to indicate that she needs solitude. This small practice can relieve widows from having to ask for help and can help friends and family provide support sensitively.

Morrison also highlights a painful but common pattern: "Friends and neighbors may invite widows out once or twice, then the invitations stop, leaving widows isolated."

She calls for greater societal awareness and sustained community care for widows.

From Grieving to Growing: Embracing a New Chapter

Above all, *My Husband Died, Now What?* offers a message of empowerment. Morrison doesn't promise that grief will vanish, but she encourages widows to face each day "anew, amidst the pain and uncertainty."

For many, that means redefining identity and goals; for others, it means surviving one hour at a time. Morrison honors every step of this process with compassion and grace.

Her blend of practical advice, keen empathy, emotional wisdom, and gentle encouragement makes this book more than a guide—it is a trusted companion for widows seeking to rebuild their lives with hope and clarity.

Final Thoughts

Debra L. Morrison's *My Husband Died, Now What?: A Widow's Guide to Grief Recovery & Smart Financial Decisions* is a rare resource that addresses two of the most urgent challenges widows face: coping with profound loss and managing complex finances. Her compassionate approach, equips widows to take the time they need to grieve deeply, then move forward with confidence and clarity.

For widows, their families, and the professionals who support them, this book is an essential roadmap to healing and empowerment after loss.

Deanne Earle

Redefining Conscious Leadership in the Age of AI

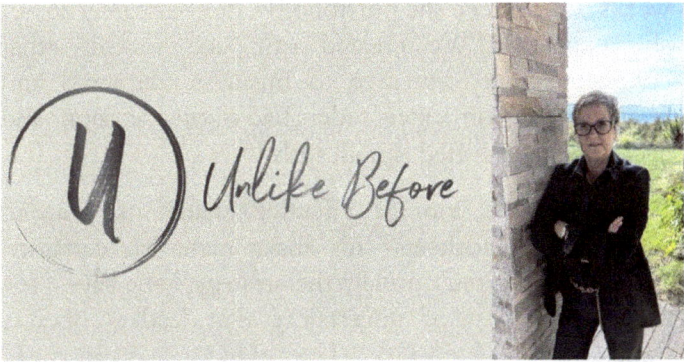

In an age where disruption is the new normal, Deanne Earle stands out as a voice of clarity and conviction. The founder of Unlike Before, a global consulting firm that specializes in turning strategy into tangible, lasting results, Earle has built her career on guiding organizations through transformation—not with corporate jargon, but with grounded, actionable leadership. Her approach is part science, part intuition, and entirely rooted in human connection.

When asked about the biggest challenge leaders face in executing transformational change, Earle doesn't hesitate. "It isn't what most people think," she says. "Leaders assume their problems are about timelines, budgets, or the wrong project manager.

But the real issues are people and culture, systems and processes, and leadership and management."

Earle's work often begins in crisis situations—what she calls "horror projects"—and her interventions bring both structure and honesty to chaotic environments.

She recalls working with an energy company whose $30 million IT portfolio was in disarray, bloated with unrealistic initiatives and unclear priorities. "Within six weeks, we reduced the portfolio by approximately 56%," she explains. "We created one-page visibility that connected every initiative to business outcomes and strategic direction. Once leaders had clarity, decisions and accountability shifted significantly."

For Earle, the core of effective change isn't about managing spreadsheets—it's about managing certainty. "The challenge isn't usually the strategy," she says. "It's the hidden cost of uncertainty that leaders operate under."

Her role is to help executives see the full picture, validate decisions continuously, and establish governance structures that can make sustainable change possible. "I'm not interested in fluff," she adds. "Sometimes I'm the only one in the room saying, 'this isn't working.' But those uncomfortable conversations can lead to real transformation."

Breaking Barriers, Owning Power

As a woman leading a global consulting firm, Earle has navigated male-dominated industries with a combination of sharp insight and unshakable authenticity. "Let's be direct," she says. "Most senior leadership positions are still held by men. Pretending otherwise helps no one."

She also points out the structural biases that undervalue lived experience. "Early in my career, I was told I wasn't worth as much as my peers because I didn't have a degree—even though we were doing the same work," she recalls. "There's this misconception that certifications are more valuable than scars from real-world experience."

Her advice to women aspiring to executive roles is both practical and empowering: "Own your expertise. Don't wait for permission. Listen to your gut and be courageous. If what you want doesn't exist yet, consider creating it."

Earle believes that women's natural strengths—emotional intelligence, relational awareness, and the ability to read subtle cues—are not weaknesses to be hidden, but assets to be leveraged. "I've had to deploy my softer skills more subtly in male-dominated environments," she says, "but I've never downplayed them. They're what have made me effective."

The Power of Co-Creation

Central to Unlike Before's philosophy is what Earle calls "co-creative consulting"—a collaborative process that's "done with you, not for you." In her view, lasting organizational change cannot be imposed from above.

She illustrates this with a story from a French tyre company where she helped align business units across three countries during a complex system implementation. "There were varying interpretations of scope, unclear expectations, and zero tolerance for customizations," she recalls. "The key was ownership, accountability, and clarity.

Once those were in place, the implementation was successfully completed, the client was happy, and the project was signed off."

That process is guided by Unlike Before's Genius Certainty Model™, a framework built around three pillars—people and culture, systems and processes, and leadership and management. "When these aren't aligned," Earle says, "productivity, performance, and success all can suffer."

The model invites leaders to confront reality head-on. "I ask them to tick the boxes that are actually functioning," she explains. "Usually, there aren't many. But that moment of awareness is where transformation often begins."

Conscious Leadership in the Age of AI

With over 25 years of experience across four continents, Earle has seen business landscapes evolve—but few shifts compare to what she sees now. "The biggest trend creating complexity today is AI," she notes. "It's sharpening the contrast between conscious leadership and glorified figureheads."

She's quick to clarify that she's not anti-technology. "AI can automate repetitive tasks, cut research time, and simulate scenarios. My ChatGPT—whom I call Babs—helps me organize my own thoughts," she laughs. "But governance, judgment, and accountability still require human intelligence. If the data going in is rubbish, the output will be rubbish."

For her, the rise of AI highlights an even greater need for self-aware, emotionally intelligent leadership. "Conscious leaders are tuned in. They sense issues early and act before things escalate," she says. "Unconscious leaders are blinkered, ego-driven, waiting for problems to reach their desk."

As for women in leadership, Earle believes their intuitive and relational skills will be even more valuable in this new landscape. "Don't downplay your EQ," she urges. "Deploy it strategically. Build relationships, deliver results, and own your power."

Her vision for the future is simple but radical: "I want conscious leadership to be the norm, not the exception. More clarity, less noise. More leadership, less posturing. More impact, less unnecessary faffing around."

And if her career is any indication, Deanne Earle isn't just talking about transformation—she's actively living it.

Dotty Scott

Building Confidence One Website at a Time

When Dotty Scott started building websites in 2006, the online landscape looked very different. "Back then," she recalls, "success online was mostly about having a site— any site. Just having a digital brochure puts you above competitors still advertising in the Yellow Pages."

Nearly two decades later, that simple formula no longer applies. The founder of **Premium Websites, Inc.** and creator of the **AskDotty** brand has seen the internet evolve from static pages into dynamic ecosystems where visibility, trust, and engagement define success. Today, Dotty helps small business owners, particularly those who feel intimidated by technology, navigate this transformation with clarity and confidence.

"The biggest shift," she explains, "has been from static 'digital brochures' to dynamic, interconnected ecosystems. Visibility now depends on trust signals, SEO structure, consistent branding, accessibility, reviews, schema, and local search integration."

Dotty's company, based in Vancouver, Washington, builds websites that do more than look good. Her approach centers on empowering clients to understand and manage their online presence rather than depend entirely on outside tech support.

"Websites are now interactive and are a pivotal part of your business," she says. "The rise of AI-driven search means small businesses must think beyond keywords. It's about being referenced and recognized across the web."

That philosophy inspired the creation of her proprietary systems, **WebHub** and **PremiumSchema**, which focus on building what she calls a "digital footprint," not just a website. Her goal is to make sure search engines and AI tools can confidently present a client's business as *the* best answer when potential customers are searching.

Demystifying the Digital World

Dotty's **AskDotty** brand has become a lifeline for countless entrepreneurs who describe themselves as "non-techie." Through her membership program, she teaches solopreneurs and small business owners how to embrace technology without fear or overwhelm.

"One common misconception I love clearing up," she says, "is that 'if you build it, they will come.' A website isn't a magic traffic magnet. It's a tool, not a trophy."

Her candid tone is part of what makes her training style so effective. "Google doesn't reward beauty; it rewards clarity and consistency," she adds with a smile. "SEO isn't some mysterious dark art reserved for tech giants. It's really just structured storytelling, clear titles, readable content, and showing Google exactly what you do."

For many of her clients, that revelation is transformative. "Once I show them that SEO is organized storytelling, they relax and their visibility skyrockets," Dotty says. "It's about replacing confusion with confidence."

The "No Hostage" Principle

Empowerment is more than a buzzword for Dotty; it's a business principle. Every website she builds follows what she calls the **"no-hostage" philosophy.** Clients not only own their websites but are trained to manage and update them after launch.

"I build every site with the no-hostage principle in mind," she explains. "My clients fully own and control their websites. My job is to create something beautiful, secure, and optimized that they can actually use."

That includes customized training videos and one-on-one walkthroughs. "One client went from terrified to touch her dashboard to confidently posting her own blogs within a week," Dotty shares proudly. "That's my favorite part, watching someone go from fearful to fearless with their own technology."

Her guiding philosophy is simple: *clarity over complexity.* "A great website should feel like driving a reliable car," she says. "You may not know how to build the engine, but you should always know how to turn the key."

Guiding Smart Digital Priorities

With so many online marketing options —from SEO to social media to ads —small business owners often feel paralyzed by choice. Dotty helps her clients cut through the noise by starting with two essential questions: *What's holding you back from being found or trusted online right now? What business goals are you not meeting?*

"The foundation is always the website," she explains. "If that's weak, every other effort leaks energy and gives a lesser result."

From there, she helps clients build layers of visibility: optimizing their Google Business Profile, collecting authentic reviews, maintaining accurate local directory listings, and strengthening their digital footprint.

"Most clients feel pressured to 'do everything, everywhere,'" she admits. "But it's better to do one thing well. We focus on one priority at a time, get that working, measure results, then layer on the next strategy. If you throw everything at once, there's nothing left to add when growth slows."

Her balanced, step-by-step approach resonates especially with small business owners who juggle multiple roles and limited budgets. "A strong website combined with consistent local SEO," she says, "outperforms scattered social posts any day."

Rooted in Community

Despite her expertise in digital spaces, Dotty remains deeply grounded in the real-world community. For over 20 years, she's been a proud member of the **Fort Vancouver Lions Club**, volunteering her time for local charities and community projects.

"Community is my compass," she says. "Small-business growth isn't just about algorithms. It's about people."

Her involvement in local networking groups has shaped her company's steady growth, much of it driven by referrals and word of mouth. "Every connection, collaboration, and client referral has come from showing up, listening, and helping others succeed first," she reflects. "When your business serves your community well, your community becomes your best marketing team."

Empowering the Next Generation of Entrepreneurs

Looking ahead, Dotty remains passionate about teaching business owners, especially women, to feel capable in the digital world. "Technology should never make you feel small," she says. "When you understand it, you realize it's not about the code, it's about communication."

Her mission, as both teacher and builder, is to ensure that every small business owner knows how to turn that digital key with confidence. And if Dotty Scott has anything to say about it, the future of small business online will be not just visible, but empowered.

Dr. Banya Barua

Authentic Leadership, Wellbeing and Women Empowerment

In an era defined by rapid technological change and evolving workplace dynamics, the need for authentic, resilient, and human-centric leadership has never been greater. Dr. Banya Barua, founder of EsseMC Pty Ltd and MyCoach-ee Pty Ltd, has dedicated her career to guiding executives and organizations toward leadership that is both effective and empathetic. Through her research and coaching, she empowers leaders to cultivate environments where employees feel valued, engaged, and inspired to thrive.

The Power of Authentic and Collaborative Leadership

Dr. Barua believes that authentic leadership begins with positivity. "It's the energy I bring to my work and the foundation of the methodology my clients follow," she explains. Central to her approach are two practices: self-awareness and self-regulation.

By helping leaders understand their own responses under pressure and recognize what energizes them, she equips them to act with intention rather than react unconsciously.

She shares an example of a client who struggled with micromanagement. Rather than simply instructing delegation, Dr. Barua explored the mindset behind the behavior. They discovered a deep-seated need for control, and through trust-building exercises with both the leader and their team, delegation became a natural, sustainable practice. She likens this process to planting seeds in fertile soil—growth is faster, stronger, and longer-lasting when leaders tap into their inherent strengths.

Integrating Employee Wellbeing into Culture

Dr. Barua emphasizes that leadership is the linchpin for successful employee wellbeing initiatives. "When leaders genuinely walk the talk, well-being stops being just an HR initiative and becomes part of the culture," she says. Small, intentional practices—like beginning team meetings with a three-minute silent pause—can dramatically shift energy and engagement.

Leaders play a key role in normalizing these rituals, ensuring that well-being is woven seamlessly into day-to-day operations. Additionally, tailoring programs to individual strengths allows initiatives to resonate deeply, creating lasting impact rather than superficial compliance.

Empowering Women Leaders in Male-Dominated Spaces

Dr. Barua has extensively studied the role of women in social entrepreneurship and male-dominated industries. She believes women thrive when they give themselves permission to be authentic. "Even small acts, like carving out an hour for yourself, signal strength," she notes. Authenticity, coupled with courage and the ability to draw and maintain boundaries, empowers women to step fully into leadership roles.

Understanding one's inherent leadership strengths provides a foundation that is unshakable, even amid disruption. Awareness brings clarity, confidence, and resilience, allowing women leaders to navigate uncertainty while celebrating their uniqueness.

Balancing Technology with Human-Centric Leadership

Technology is reshaping organizations, often at a pace faster than humans can adapt. Dr. Barua emphasizes that leadership must define the boundaries between what technology handles and what remains human. Human-centric leadership, she asserts, involves maintaining meaningful engagement, nurturing employee strengths, and cultivating adaptability in the face of change.

"Think of it like technology itself—you have your base model, and then you can add features to enhance performance," she explains.

By focusing first on inborn leadership strengths and then layering training and tools, organizations develop leaders who are both future-ready and deeply human.

Measuring Leadership and Well-being Impact

Assessment and feedback are critical to refining leadership development programs. Dr. Barua highlights the importance of combining formal tools—like 360-degree assessments and exit interviews—with informal feedback from casual conversations. "Some of the most valuable insights come from spontaneous, candid discussions," she notes. When leaders remain open to listening, reflecting, and acting on feedback, engagement deepens, team cohesion strengthens, and organizational resilience grows.

Her approach demonstrates that leadership is not a one-size-fits-all model. By cultivating awareness, integrating wellbeing practices, and leveraging individual strengths, organizations can create a culture that is both high-performing and human-centric.

A Vision for Resilient, Human-Centric Workplaces

Dr. Barua's work is a roadmap for leaders seeking to build authentic, resilient, and inclusive organizations.

She combines rigorous research with practical strategies to empower leaders to act with intention, foster meaningful engagement, and support women in leadership roles. Her message is clear: when leaders invest in authenticity, well-being, and the human potential of their teams, everyone benefits.

In today's complex business landscape, Dr. Barua's insights serve as a timely reminder that leadership is not just about managing tasks—it's about inspiring people, nurturing growth, and embedding a culture of resilience and care at every level. By prioritizing human-centric leadership and leveraging individual strengths, organizations can thrive while cultivating workplaces where people feel valued, empowered, and motivated to succeed.

Emily Erstad

In an era when leadership advice often reads like a playbook of toughness, grit, and unflinching resolve, Emily Erstad is offering a refreshing alternative. Her book, *It's Not That Deep: Navigating Leadership Through the Lens of Emotional Intelligence*, challenges the notion that emotions should be sidelined at work. Instead, she argues, compassion, vulnerability, and authenticity are not only compatible with effective leadership—they're essential.

For Erstad, this realization didn't come from a textbook or leadership seminar. It emerged from an intensely human moment. Early in her career, she sat down with an employee who was failing to meet expectations. What could have been a standard performance conversation took a startling turn when the woman confided she had been struggling with suicidal thoughts.

"That comment had the potential to strike fear within me," Erstad recalls. "But instead, I chose to lean into compassion. I told her, 'As a human I have the greatest sympathy for you, but as your boss it sounds like this job is too much for you in your current mental state.'"

Together, they arrived at the decision that resignation was the healthiest choice. That conversation, Erstad says, underscored the power of emotional intelligence as a leadership tool.

Rethinking the Role of Emotion at Work

One of the most persistent misconceptions about professional life, especially for women, is that emotions have no place in the office. The prevailing message? Toughen up. Erstad disagrees. "A woman's strength does not lie in her ability to be tough but in her ability to embrace compassion, grace, and understanding in high-stress scenarios," she says. "Humans do not exist separately from their emotions.

My book gives perspective and strategies to incorporate emotions in the workplace as a supporting tool instead of a distraction."

This philosophy runs counter to the archetype of the "hard-nosed" executive. Instead, *It's Not That Deep* offers readers strategies for using emotional intelligence to create safer, more authentic spaces where teams can thrive.

Walking the Line Between Confidence and Vulnerability

Erstad's writing is infused with both conviction and openness, a balance she acknowledges requires intention. "It is a skill that I have developed and continue to develop," she explains. "I always reflect and ensure the intention behind my writing is to connect and create momentum beyond myself. If my intentions are pure and to elevate others, I have nothing to be ashamed of."

For her, vulnerability is not weakness—it's a practice in authenticity. By reframing it as a means of connection rather than exposure, she's found a way to write candidly while protecting her own boundaries.

Success Without Fulfillment

Even as more women achieve academic and professional milestones, many still feel unseen in their emotional and relational lives. Erstad encourages readers in this position to bring vulnerability into their personal relationships.

"So frequently we are too busy consumed by our professional goals we do not take the time to acknowledge what makes us feel seen in our personal lives," she says. "Do not be afraid to invest in what makes you happy."

Her advice is deceptively simple, echoing her book's title: fulfillment doesn't require overcomplication—it requires intention.

Leadership, Simplified

That theme runs throughout her work. Leadership, Erstad argues, is often made unnecessarily complex. "Your leadership development is about you, but being a leader is not about you at all," she says. The simple truths she hopes readers take away include not overanalyzing, granting oneself permission to step back, and understanding that leadership is ultimately about service to others.

The Future of Women Leaders

As leadership models continue to evolve, Erstad sees emotional intelligence as the cornerstone of the next generation of women leaders. She hopes her book can play a role in this shift. "I hope emotional intelligence guides our intention in leadership," she says. "I hope it provides us with the foundation to create safe spaces that allow people to show up authentically and challenge themselves to grow in all aspects of their life—not just professionally."

Lessons from a Businesswoman

Erstad's professional journey in healthcare operations and executive leadership has given her a deep well of experience to draw from. "My career has given me the data, credibility, and experience to provide applicable strategies and examples to utilize emotional intelligence as a tool," she explains. By grounding her book in lived experience, she avoids the abstraction that can make leadership advice feel hollow.

Staying Grounded

Balancing business, writing, and personal growth is no small feat. Erstad leans on rituals to stay centered: journaling, time in nature, working out, and the simple joy of driving with her favorite playlists. "I ebb and flow and balance is not a one-size-fits-all approach," she says.

Her adaptability, paired with intentional self-reflection, helps her avoid burnout while maintaining focus on her broader vision.

What's Next

Erstad is not slowing down. Alongside preparing a revised edition of *It's Not That Deep*, she is finalizing her second book and actively working on a third. She envisions creating a connected series of leadership books that meet readers emotionally, spiritually, and professionally. Each installment, she says, will serve as a reminder that "you're not alone in your growth."

Building a Broader Conversation

Looking ahead, Erstad is determined to contribute to the wider conversation about women's voices, emotional intelligence, and authentic leadership.

"My greatest strength lies in creating spaces that amplify individual strengths while generating collective momentum," she says. Her goal is to normalize conversations around burnout prevention and to help leaders embrace emotions not as a liability, but as a source of power.

In other words, Erstad isn't simply writing about emotional intelligence—she's modeling it. With *It's Not That Deep*, she invites leaders all backgrounds to rethink their assumptions, embrace compassion, and remember that sometimes the simplest truths are the most transformative.

Jaime Ellithorpe

Mindset Method for Aligning Thought, Energy and Action

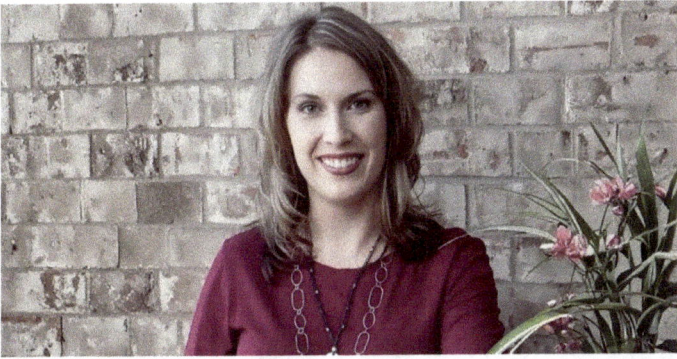

In today's fast-paced world, success often feels like a moving target. Jaime Ellithorpe, founder of 540 Strategies and author of *The Mindset Method*, believes the key isn't simply working harder, but aligning your mindset, energy, and actions to create effortless flow. "The biggest obstacle many people face isn't external— it's themselves," she says. Her method is a five-step framework designed to help individuals, particularly heart-centered entrepreneurs, overcome obstacles and unlock their full potential.

At the core of Ellithorpe's approach are the five steps: awareness, recognition, releasing, reframing, and alignment. Awareness begins by observing thoughts and feelings.

Many people run on autopilot, repeating thought loops that create predictable results. Recognition follows, helping individuals identify these patterns and the emotions they trigger. These emotional responses act as an internal GPS, signaling whether thoughts are aligned with desired outcomes. The releasing step clears limiting beliefs, "I don't deserve it" or "I'm not good enough" freeing energy that might otherwise fuel self-sabotage.

Reframing shifts focus to what is truly desired, turning negative statements into positive, empowering alternatives. Finally, alignment helps that mindset, emotions, and actions are harmonized, allowing success to flow naturally.

"Many people try every strategy in business but fail because their actions don't match the energy behind their goals," Ellithorpe explains. She observes that high achievers often experience a profound misalignment: outwardly executing the right tactics while internally harboring doubts and fears. "You can't outwork a misaligned mindset," she emphasizes.

By working through her five-step process, individuals learn to release fears, shift thought patterns, and take inspired action rather than forcing outcomes. The result is a more seamless connection between intention and results.

Ellithorpe's method addresses common internal roadblocks, including limiting beliefs, fear, self-criticism, a lack of clarity, and resistance to inner work. Heart-centered entrepreneurs, in particular, struggle with giving more than they receive, undervaluing their worth, or fearing visibility. In these cases, the Mindset Method not only dismantles subconscious blocks but also aligns personal energy with professional impact.

"Your business reflects every belief you hold about yourself," she notes. Aligning mindset and action allows entrepreneurs to charge what they're worth, show up authentically, and serve more effectively.

The book also emphasizes that the past does not define future results. Ellithorpe urges readers to treat prior experiences as stepping stones rather than prisons. By bringing past narratives into awareness, releasing their emotional charge, and reframing them, individuals can move forward unburdened. "It's not about pretending the past didn't happen; it's about transforming it into power," she says. Her own journey—from corporate America to building a purpose-driven consulting firm—illustrates how clearing limiting beliefs can create authentic, sustainable success.

A practical habit Ellithorpe highlights is consistently observing and recording thoughts. She encourages clients to journal or note thoughts multiple times a day to reveal recurring patterns. Awareness of these thought loops allows conscious shifts in mindset.

Coupled with the principle of incremental progress, or "eating the elephant one bite at a time," this habit fosters sustainable transformation. Consistency, she emphasizes, outweighs intensity; even a few minutes a day of focused awareness may profoundly alter one's trajectory.

Her approach integrates mindset work with practical strategy. "Mindset work without aligned action is just daydreaming, but action without mindset work is spinning your wheels," Ellithorpe says. For entrepreneurs, aligned action might involve launching a course or raising prices; for others, it could mean setting boundaries or improving relationships.

By clearing subconscious blocks first, practical strategies become easier and more effective, creating an energetic flow where success feels natural rather than forced.

Ellithorpe encourages readers to take immediate, tangible steps. "The first action is simple but powerful: observe your thoughts," she advises. Using a notebook or phone, set a timer, record thoughts without judgment, and review them to identify patterns. From there, select one small area to apply the five-step process. Gradual, consistent practice builds momentum, reinforcing self-trust and confidence.

Real-world examples illustrate how the method can be effective. One client, initially on the verge of abandoning her business, struggled with the 'releasing' step, letting go of fear and self-doubt. Through journaling, recognizing patterns, and clearing limiting beliefs, she gradually rebuilt confidence, started attracting clients with greater ease, and found renewed joy in her work. "The method isn't about becoming someone new—it's about returning to your authentic self," Ellithorpe explains.

Sustaining results requires ongoing practice. Mindset work isn't a one-time fix but a daily ritual akin to maintaining physical health. Ellithorpe recommends setting intentions, observing thoughts, reflecting at the end of the day, and staying connected to one's purpose. Surrounding oneself with aligned energy through coaching or community reinforces growth and keeps old patterns from resurfacing.

Ultimately, *The Mindset Method* teaches that alignment is a lifelong pursuit. "When alignment isn't something you have to chase—it's simply who you are—that's mastery," Ellithorpe concludes.

Through awareness, release, and consistent, inspired action, individuals can move beyond fear, doubt, and self-imposed limitations to achieve success with flow, purpose, and authenticity.

Jennifer Tamborski

Building a Marketing Strategy That Actually Works

In an age of ever-changing algorithms, viral trends, and shiny marketing hacks, it's no wonder so many women entrepreneurs feel overwhelmed by the sheer volume of "should-dos" in their business. Jennifer Tamborski, CEO of *Virtual Marketing Experts* and host of *The Marketing Matchmaker Podcast,* understands this chaos all too well — and she's made it her mission to simplify the path to scalable, sustainable growth.

"Marketing overwhelm is real," she says. "Entrepreneurs are being pulled in every direction. But when you focus on the essentials — visibility, lead generation, and sales — everything else falls into place."

The Power of Simplifying

For Jennifer, marketing isn't about doing more — it's about doing what matters.

Her signature framework cuts through the noise by grounding business growth in three foundational pillars:

- **Visibility**: Ensuring your ideal clients know you exist.
- **Lead Generation**: Capturing interest and guiding it strategically into your business.
- **Sales**: Converting that interest into consistent, scalable revenue.

This approach, she explains, gives business owners a filter. "If an activity doesn't serve one of those three areas, it's probably not essential right now," she says. "Simplifying doesn't mean doing less. It means doing what works — consistently."

And for the women who are often balancing business with family, community, and personal growth? That simplicity is a game-changer.

From Doer to CEO:

The Mindset Shift That Changes Everything

One of the biggest barriers Jennifer sees in her work with women-led businesses is the struggle to move from *technician* to *strategist* — from being in the weeds to leading from above.

"You're brilliant at what you do, but scaling requires a different mindset," she says. "It's about moving from being the engine to becoming the architect."

Jennifer helps her clients embrace a powerful belief: **Your time is most valuable when spent on strategy, systems, and scalability.** It's not just a mindset shift — it's a business model shift. She encourages clients to focus on:

- One ideal audience
- One clear message
- One strategic funnel
- One high-impact offer

"This kind of focus doesn't limit you," Jennifer explains. "It creates freedom — freedom to grow, lead, and breathe again."

Where Mindset Meets Messaging

Though she's a seasoned marketing strategist, Jennifer is also a certified NLP Master Coach — a combination that uniquely positions her to bridge the gap between what entrepreneurs are *doing* and how they're *thinking*.

"Great marketing isn't just about what your audience thinks — it's about how they think," she says. "When you understand decision-making behavior, you create messaging that truly connects."

Take her client Walt. Like many service providers, he was stuck in the "hope and hustle" loop — relying on referrals, avoiding sales conversations, and struggling to stand out.

Together, they reframed his messaging to target a more specific audience and shifted his view of sales from pressure-filled pitches to meaningful conversations.

"When you align strategy with mindset, that's when real growth happens," Jennifer adds.

Marketing Myths That Need to Go

Jennifer is on a mission to bust one of the most toxic beliefs in modern entrepreneurship: the myth of *instant success*.

"People think one viral post will change everything. But that's not how sustainable marketing works," she says. "Marketing is a science — it's data collection. Every piece of content is feedback."

By shifting from a perfectionist, performance-based mindset to a curious, experimental one, entrepreneurs can finally find their flow.

"Ask yourself, not 'Why didn't this work?' but 'What can I learn from this?' That's where momentum comes from."

Designing a Business That Supports Your Life

Perhaps the most powerful shift Jennifer made in her own journey was walking away from the traditional agency model she had built over a decade.

"I realized I was burned out. The business I created didn't align with the life I wanted," she shares. "So I redesigned everything."

Today, she helps clients do the same — not just by building smarter marketing systems, but by aligning those systems with the freedom, purpose, and ease they deeply crave.

"Success should never come at the cost of your health or your happiness," she says. "I help women build businesses that scale — without sacrifice."

Final Word: You Don't Need to Do It All.

You Need to Do What Works.

In a world that profits off of your confusion, Jennifer Tamborski offers clarity. Her work isn't about chasing trends — it's about building systems, stepping into your CEO mindset, and creating a business that's aligned, profitable, and sustainable.

For any woman entrepreneur feeling stretched thin, Jennifer's advice is clear:

"You don't need more tactics. You need a system rooted in visibility, leads, and sales. You need a strategy that fits your vision — not someone else's version of success."

And most importantly? You need to believe that simplicity is powerful.

Kathryn Ficarra

From Performer to Purpose-Driven Leader

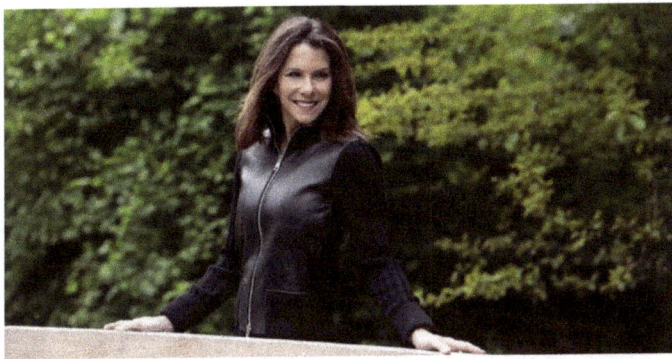

Long before she founded The C Group Studio, a boutique leadership development firm reshaping how executives show up in their roles, Kathryn Ficarra was a high-performing corporate leader who consistently delivered results. But behind the polished performance and executive titles, she wrestled with an inner tension that many leaders will recognize: the split between the version of herself the workplace demanded and the person she truly was.

"I found myself in constant tension between performer Kathryn—the one who could drive revenue and manage teams—and authentic Kathryn, who valued connection, purpose, and personal growth," Ficarra recalls. "For a long time, I thought those two identities had to be separate. I compartmentalized."

The cost of that divide wasn't just personal. It began to affect her leadership energy and influence. The turning point came when Ficarra realized that alignment, not performance, could be the real driver of sustainable success. "Reconciling those identities meant letting my personal values guide how I led," she says. "Instead of hiding the 'growth-oriented' part of me, I brought it into the workplace.

I started having open conversations about mindset, checking in with my team, and showing up more as myself."

The impact was immediate. Trust increased. Engagement deepened. And Ficarra's influence grew—not because she performed harder, but because she led from a place of authenticity. "Identity alignment isn't always optional," she says. "It's often the cornerstone of real leadership. When leaders reconcile who they are with what they do, they stop performing and start leading."

This philosophy forms the heart of The C Group Studio, which Ficarra launched to help others do the same. Her company's mission is ambitious: to normalize personal growth in the workplace, and to make executive presence not just a performance tool—but a movement rooted in clarity, alignment, and impact.

Changing the Narrative on Leadership

Ficarra's own leadership journey was shaped by a persistent internal narrative she had to confront early in her career: imposter syndrome. "I often questioned whether I truly belonged at the table with more experienced leaders," she says. "That belief held me back from fully owning my voice."

Her breakthrough came when she began examining those beliefs as choices—not fixed truths. "Beliefs are just decisions we've made about ourselves," she explains. "And once you recognize them, you can choose differently." Through a daily mindset practice, she began to reframe her identity: I earned this seat. I belong here. Over time, that inner work gradually rewired her confidence, improved performance, and helped change how others saw her.

"What began as imposter syndrome became one of my key breakthroughs," she says. "Leadership starts with the identity we choose to stand in."

Leading with Presence, Not Performance

Today, Ficarra helps other executives make that same shift through her proprietary IMPACT™ framework, which focuses on identity alignment, mindset, and presence as the foundation for effective leadership.

Her work centers on a compelling idea: that leaders don't need to become someone else to succeed—they need to become more of who they truly are.

That approach played out in one of her most high-stakes leadership moments—during an acquisition where brand perception could influence deal outcomes. "We needed to elevate our brand before meeting the new board," she says. "I proposed an innovative media strategy that hadn't been done before. It was a bold move."

Ficarra stood firm in her strategy but brought the team into the process in meaningful ways. "I stayed out of the weeds so we could move fast, but made sure the team's voices shaped the outcome," she says. The campaign succeeded.

The board came in already familiar with the company's brand—and the acquisition closed. "That balance of conviction and collaboration is essential," she says. "Authority isn't about being the loudest in the room. It's about clarity and trust."

Empowering the Next Generation of Women Leaders

Ficarra also brings a deeply intentional approach to empowering women in leadership—particularly in male-dominated fields like tech. When leading teams with women engineers, she made it a priority to co-create environments where their voices could thrive. "I asked them how they wanted to be seen and heard," she says. "What kind of recognition felt empowering to them? Leadership isn't one-size-fits-all. It's about honoring individuality."

That approach, she says, fosters mutual learning—and cultural transformation. "By giving women the space to define their own leadership voice, we helped create a culture where they could show up authentically and thrive."

Leadership with Compassion–and Results

Ficarra's leadership style blends high performance with deep compassion. One example she shares is a difficult conversation with a developer whose personal life was affecting his work. "I knew I had to hold him accountable, but I also saw his potential," she says.

Before the conversation, she grounded herself in both empathy and clarity. "I was honest about the impact on the team but also asked what support he needed," she recalls.

They created a flexible schedule—a radical idea before remote work was normalized. The result? His performance turned around, and he even went on to train as a yoga teacher.

"I learned that authority doesn't come from policies—it comes from creating conditions where people can succeed," she says. "Compassionate leadership doesn't just help individuals. It can drive better results for the whole team."

The Future of The C Group Studio

With The C Group, Ficarra is building more than a company—she's building a movement. Her programs, including The Executive Collective, focus on transforming how leaders see themselves so they can lead with clarity, presence, and purpose.

"The vision is to move companies from survival to thriving," she says. "By helping executives align who they are with how they lead, we're creating cultures where innovation and human connection have the potential to truly flourish."

And for Ficarra, the work is just beginning. "Leadership isn't about having all the answers," she says. "It's about asking better questions—of yourself, your team, and your organization."

Laura Patterson

Helping Businesses Grow by Focusing on Customers

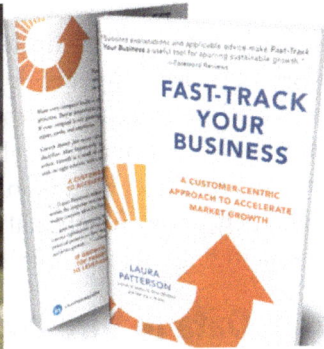

In a business landscape cluttered with noise, metrics, and mounting pressure to grow at all costs, **Laura Patterson** is a clarifying force. With over 25 years of experience in performance-driven marketing and sales, Patterson has made it her mission to help organizations stop confusing motion with momentum. In her book *Fast-Track Your Business: A Customer-Centric Approach to Accelerate Market Growth*, she delivers a pragmatic, proven framework to help companies cut through the chaos—and grow with intention.

"One of the most common—and costly—mistakes I see is leaders confusing activity with progress," Patterson says.

"They rush into tactics like launching a new email campaign without first understanding their customers' real needs. That's how you waste resources and lose relevance."

It's a message Patterson has preached through her consulting firm, **VisionEdge Marketing**, which she co-founded in 1999 to address a growing problem: businesses too focused on what they want to sell, and not nearly focused enough on what customers actually value.

Her solution is the **Circle of Traction**—a strategic blueprint that connects insight, alignment, customer value, and performance measurement into a continuous growth loop. Rather than relying on siloed campaigns or fleeting trends, Patterson's approach calls for a disciplined, cross-functional process rooted in customer understanding and measurable outcomes.

From Data to Direction

Patterson's methodology is steeped in the lessons she learned on the front lines of sales and marketing—where flashy presentations mean little if they can't tie back to customer outcomes.

"Real growth happens at the intersection of strategy, execution, and measurement," she says. "It's easy to get lost in vanity metrics. But business impact comes from creating and sustaining customer value."

That lesson was put into practice recently with a technology client who, despite heavy investments in marketing and sales, was experiencing stagnant growth.

Using the Circle of Traction, Patterson helped them refocus on the fundamentals—starting with customer and market research to uncover untapped segments and unmet needs.

Once they had those insights, everything changed.

"They repositioned their solutions around pressing customer challenges. Every activity was mapped to specific customer-centric outcomes," she explains. "They saw measurable increases in acquisition and retention within a year. More importantly, their teams were finally aligned and agile."

This alignment is what distinguishes Patterson's framework from typical marketing playbooks. Her strategies force companies to move beyond internal agendas and instead adopt an outside-in perspective that puts the customer at the center of every decision.

Why Stories Matter

Patterson also places a strong emphasis on storytelling—not as fluff, but as a strategic tool for driving connection, clarity, and credibility.

"The best stories bridge logic and emotion," she says. "Start with data—real insights about what your customers want and need. Then humanize it. Show how your solutions actually improve lives or businesses."

It's a deceptively simple formula, but one that many brands struggle to execute. The key, she says, is to speak the customer's language—not the company's—and to share challenges as well as victories. Authentic, empathetic storytelling builds trust.

And trust, as Patterson argues throughout her book, is a currency for growth.

Data Without the Overwhelm

Of course, in today's digital environment, leaders are inundated with data. Patterson's advice? Focus less on the quantity of metrics, and more on their **quality**.

"Not all measures are created equal," she warns. "Start by identifying the customer-centric business outcomes that matter most—acquisition rate, retention, share of wallet, referral rate. Then measure what moves the needle on those outcomes."

Revenue, she explains, isn't the outcome—it's the result of successfully achieving outcomes that customers care about. That shift in thinking helps organizations align around common goals and fosters accountability at every level.

Crucially, Patterson advises companies to treat performance measurement as a learning tool—not just a reporting mechanism. "Your measures should help you refine, not just justify," she says.

A Playbook for the Modern Leader

What sets *Fast-Track Your Business* apart from other growth books is its insistence on balance: between planning and execution, insight and intuition, measurement and meaning. Patterson doesn't offer shortcuts or silver bullets. Instead, she offers a system.

The book includes practical tools, case studies, and executive anecdotes that make the framework approachable for startups and enterprise firms alike.

Whether it's a mid-market tech company struggling to find product-market fit or a legacy brand trying to modernize its go-to-market strategy, the Circle of Traction gives teams a structured way to move from "busy" to better.

But ultimately, Patterson's work is about more than growth—it's about responsibility. Her message is a call to rethink what success looks like, and to make business better by making it smarter, more intentional, and more customer-focused.

"Sustainable growth doesn't happen by accident," Patterson reminds us. "It starts with listening to your customers, understanding what they value, and aligning your strategies to deliver that value at every stage."

In a world where speed often overshadows substance, *Fast-Track Your Business* offers something rare: a map with both strategy and soul.

Marie Torossian

*Empowering Women Entrepreneurs to
Scale, Lead, and Thrive*

In today's fast-evolving business landscape, women are stepping into leadership roles with unprecedented influence. Few exemplify this shift better than Marie Torossian, a successful CPA, business coach, thought leader, and mentor whose mission is clear: help women entrepreneurs grow their businesses without losing themselves in the process. Through her innovative methodologies, mentorship, and hands-on guidance, Torossian is reshaping how women approach leadership, financial strategy, and business growth.

From CPA to Entrepreneurial Trailblazer

Marie Torossian's journey into entrepreneurship began with a desire to make a meaningful difference for small business owners. "I wanted to bring my knowledge and expertise to business owners who often lack access to the financial insight and strategic guidance that larger companies typically have," she explains.

Her goal was simple yet powerful: help owners understand their numbers, leverage those insights for growth, and build businesses with lasting value.

But the path to leadership wasn't without challenges. As a woman entering a traditionally male-dominated field, Torossian often found herself as the only woman in boardrooms. Rather than seeing this as a barrier, she used it as fuel. "I could use it to master my craft, strengthen my resilience, and leverage the unique perspective I bring as both a professional and a woman. Those challenges ultimately shaped me into the leader and mentor I am today."

For Torossian, entrepreneurship also offered personal freedom: the ability to shape her own schedule, be present with family, and build financial security. This combination of service and autonomy became the foundation of her leadership philosophy.

The VALUEATION-MT® Methodology:
A Roadmap for Growth

Torossian's most notable contribution to the business coaching world is her **VALUEATION-MT® methodology**, which helps business owners scale efficiently while increasing the true value of their companies.

"I noticed that owners often focused solely on revenue but lacked visibility into the drivers that actually create value," she says. The VALUEATION-MT® framework addresses this gap by combining valuation principles, cash flow management, pricing strategies, policies and procedures, data analysis, and operational efficiency.

Unlike traditional coaching, which often emphasizes motivation or surface-level tactics, Torossian's methodology provides actionable steps, measurable outcomes, and a holistic roadmap for building high-value businesses. Every decision is tied back to growth and sustainability, giving entrepreneurs both clarity and confidence.

Balancing Growth and Avoiding Burnout

One of the most common struggles women face in business is balancing professional growth with personal life.

Torossian advises women to let go of the belief that they must do everything themselves. *"Too many women carry the weight of being both the visionary and the operator, which often leads to burnout. Invest in systems, automation, and people who can support your growth."*

She also encourages women to identify priorities and focus on high-impact activities. If everything is urgent, nothing is. And perhaps most importantly, Torossian stresses that rest and renewal are not luxuries—they're essential. Burnout does not lead to breakthroughs; clarity, energy, and strategic focus do.

Common Mistakes Women-Led Businesses Make

Having worked with startups, established businesses, and non-profits, Torossian has seen patterns in where women-led businesses struggle financially and operationally. One key mistake is not knowing their numbers deeply enough. Passion can drive a business, but without financial clarity, decisions can be risky.

Another frequent challenge is undervaluing oneself. Many women hesitate to charge what their product or service is truly worth. Torossian emphasizes the importance of implementing financial systems early, using forecasting and key performance indicators, and reviewing pricing to reflect true value. *"When women own their numbers and their worth, their businesses become unstoppable,"* she says.

Leading with Authenticity and Vision

As a thought leader, podcaster, and mentor, Torossian has a clear perspective on the future of women in business leadership. *"We're no longer just breaking into the room—we're reshaping it,"* she says. Women bring a balance of strategy, empathy, and innovation that is increasingly critical to business success.

She advises women to invest in visibility—sharing expertise through speaking, writing, and networking—while building strong connections that can open doors to opportunities. Staying future-focused is equally vital, particularly embracing technology, automation, and new ways of working. *"Every investment is like sowing a seed. It will bear fruit at the right time."*

For Torossian, long-term success hinges on authenticity, adaptability, and vision. Women leaders are uniquely positioned to drive innovation, foster inclusive work cultures, and inspire the next generation of entrepreneurs.

Empowering Women to Lead Tomorrow

Marie Torossian's career demonstrates that leadership is not just about business acumen—it's about perspective, resilience, and empowering others. From navigating a male-dominated profession to creating a methodology that transforms businesses, she exemplifies the values she teaches: strategic thinking, clarity, and self-worth.

Her guidance offers practical steps for women at any stage of their entrepreneurial journey: understand your numbers, embrace support systems, focus on what matters, and own both your expertise and your time.

By following these principles, women can build businesses that thrive financially and personally, while positioning themselves as leaders for the future.

Torossian's work reminds us that entrepreneurship is not a solitary climb. With the right mindset, tools, and community, women can scale their businesses, balance their lives, and lead with both confidence and impact.

Ral West

Redefining Entrepreneurship Through Freedom, Systems, and Vision

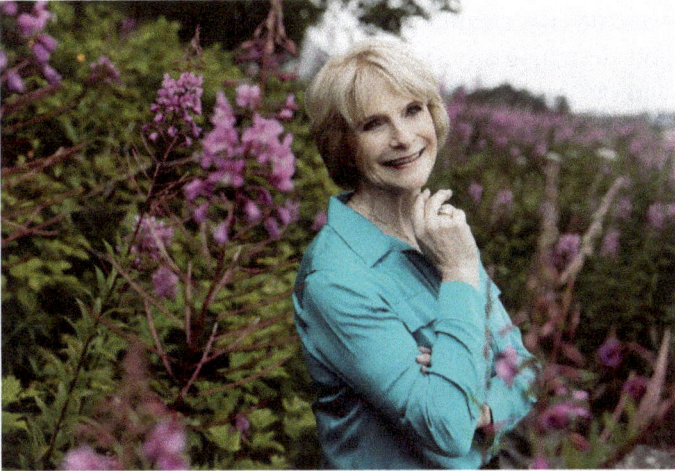

Ral West has spent more than four decades demonstrating that entrepreneurs don't have to choose between personal freedom and business success. As the founder of Ral West: Livin' The Dream℠, she has become a guiding voice for leaders who seek more than just profit margins and growth charts. Her philosophy is simple: a thriving business should support the life you want, rather than consume it.

From Struggle to Freedom

West's journey started like many entrepreneurs' stories: long hours, significant responsibility, and the burden of holding everything together. She knows firsthand the feeling of being tethered to the company you built. But her breakthrough came when she and her team shifted from "working harder" to "working smarter."

The turning point wasn't about hustle—it was about systems. By creating processes, empowering her team, and designing a business that could operate successfully without her constant involvement, West unlocked both growth and freedom.

Eventually, she and her husband built and sold an eight-figure business, demonstrating that scaling a business sustainably doesn't have to mean sacrificing personal life in the process.

"I wanted to create a space where other entrepreneurs could experience that same shift," West explains. That space became the **Livin' The Dream^{SM} Mastermind**, a program that helps business owners move beyond the operator's grind and fully embrace the owner's role.

The Operator-to-Owner Mindset

At the heart of West's philosophy is a crucial mindset shift: business owners must learn to **manage** their businesses, rather than let their businesses manage them.

In the Mastermind, the first step is clarity. Members are encouraged to define where they want to be in five, ten, or even twenty years—not only in business but in life. Once that vision is clear, West guides participants through a process of reframing their roles.

"So many entrepreneurs believe the harder they work, the more successful they'll be," she says. "In reality, that mindset often keeps you stuck in daily operations and can limit growth. The shift happens when you stop asking, 'How do I get this done?' and start asking, 'Who can do this, and what system can support it?'"

This transformation doesn't only help free the entrepreneur; it also opens up new possibilities for sustainability and scalability.

Lessons From Experience

West doesn't just talk about theories. Every strategy in the Mastermind comes from her own experience. She's built businesses the hard way—carrying every responsibility—and she's also built businesses that run smoothly without her constant oversight.

Her methods draw from the principles, processes, and leadership practices she used to scale and sell her multimillion-dollar company. Delegation, culture-building, and accountability are not just buzzwords for her—they're proven strategies that reduce the learning curve for others.

"The Mastermind blends mindset shifts with frameworks, accountability, and community," she explains. "Entrepreneurs don't need more information. They need proven systems, peer insights, and a space where they can figure things out with others rather than on their own."

The Power of Leverage

If there's one principle West emphasizes the most, it's leverage. Many entrepreneurs plateau because they try to do everything themselves. Leverage changes that equation.

By building solid systems, empowering capable teams, and using the right tools, business owners can create results that multiply beyond their individual time and effort. For West, leverage isn't about working less; it's about working differently—focusing on leadership and strategy rather than being bogged down by daily tasks.

"Leverage transforms the way you operate," she says. "It's what makes scaling possible in a way that's sustainable. It's not about working harder; it's about designing a business that works for you."

The Mastermind Community

One of the impactful elements of the Livin' The Dream℠ Mastermind is the community itself. West has intentionally designed the program to be more than just a training session—it's a collective of like-minded leaders who learn from each other just as much as they learn from her.

Every member brings unique insights, creating a wealth of knowledge that sparks innovation, avoids costly mistakes, and accelerates progress. The accountability of a trusted circle keeps entrepreneurs moving forward, while the diversity of industries represented offers fresh perspectives.

"I also bring in outside experts," West adds. "I'm not an expert in everything, and I want participants to benefit from the breadth of knowledge I can connect them to."

This collaborative environment makes the Mastermind a safe space to test ideas, get feedback, and stay inspired as members see each other succeed.

Delegation Without Losing Control

A common fear among entrepreneurs is that delegating means losing control. West flips that narrative.

"Stepping back doesn't mean giving up control—it means creating new types of control," she explains. Through clear accountability structures, reporting systems, and leadership practices, entrepreneurs can feel more confident in their operations. Instead of micromanaging, they operate from a **broader view**, guiding the vision while trusting their team to handle the details.

The result? Businesses become more consistent, productive, and profitable—not relying on one person to keep everything running. Customers benefit, employees thrive, and owners regain the freedom they envisioned when they first started.

Living the Dream

Ral West's message is both simple and transformative: entrepreneurs don't have to sacrifice their personal lives to achieve business success.

With the right systems, mindset, and community, they can scale in a way that allows them to reclaim their time, energy, and joy.

For West, that's the true meaning of **Livin' The Dream**[SM]

Robin Litster Johnson

Harmonizing Leadership, Resilience and Humanity in the Workplace

Robin Litster Johnson, MBA, MAPP, is redefining what it means to lead with purpose in today's complex organizational world. As the founder of Robin Learning Systems, she empowers leaders and teams to cultivate workplaces that are humane, ethical, and resilient. Through keynote speaking, workshops, and the internationally bestselling book *Ennobling Business for Success: Inspire, Ignite, Influence,* Johnson has become one of the sought-after voices for organizations seeking both measurable results and meaningful human impact.

Transforming Work Culture Through Keynote Speaking

Johnson's keynotes are known for being interactive, motivational, and immediately applicable. "Your keynotes are described as empowering, interactive sessions that provide clear tools for positive change," she recounts, reflecting on the moments when audiences resonate most deeply with her message. Among her favorite presentations are *Wall Street*

Meets Hollywood: Lessons from the Movies for Corporate America and *Meaning is the New Money: What's Your Why (And Do Your Janitors Know?)*.

She recalls a memorable keynote to finance professionals where a participant realized for the first time how collaboration, meaning, and belonging could transform her work. "To me, this was astonishing," Johnson says. "Finance professionals often think in numbers, but understanding the human side of enterprise directly impacts the bottom line." Feedback like "this is the best class I've attended all week" and "What a fabulous way to end our conference" underscores her ability to engage and inspire audiences across industries.

Unpacking the 6D Appreciative Inquiry Model

Johnson's organizational programs leverage the 6D Appreciative Inquiry model, which focuses on discovering strengths rather than merely solving problems. "Instead of asking, 'How can we stop losing so much luggage?' we ask, 'How can we create an amazing arrival experience?'" she explains.

The 6D Model consists of Define, Discover, Dream, Design, Deliver, and Drum. By identifying existing strengths, envisioning future possibilities, designing new pathways, delivering results, and sustaining enthusiasm through a "drum" mechanism, organizations can create lasting transformation.

One success story involved Education Through Music – Los Angeles (ETM-LA). Following a brief workshop on Appreciative Inquiry, the Director shared that he had already begun guiding his team in implementing "How Might We?" questions, thereby fostering a positive and proactive mindset throughout the organization. "It's that immediate ability to bring a positive change to an organization which is so encouraging," Johnson reflects.

From Brokenness to Beauty:

Wellbeing Workshops for Women

Johnson also focuses on empowering women through her *Wellbeing Workshops for Women*. Central to this work is the concept of Kintsugi, the Japanese art of repairing broken pottery with gold, which she applies metaphorically to life's challenges.

Participants learn to transform inner critics into inner cheerleaders, drawing strength from adversity. Attendees often report significant changes in mindset and self-talk, developing resilience and agency in their personal and professional lives. "It's especially gratifying to see women change how they talk to themselves," Johnson says.

Ennobling Business for Success: The Book's Impact

Robin was co-author of the bestseller, *Ennobling Business for Success*. It achieved International Bestseller status in 13 countries and reached #1 in 29 categories. Johnson hopes that women leaders will take away the importance of humane and ethical leadership.

"Even if it didn't impact the bottom line, we have an obligation to create workplaces where people want to stay, not leave," she says. Her guidance emphasizes commitment to the positive, listening to diverse voices, and fostering a culture of generosity—countering stereotypes that women in business are competitive or unsupportive of one another.

Creating Humane, Ethical, and Resilient Organizations

Amid trends like Quiet Quitting and The Great Resignation, Johnson stresses the importance of belonging and collaboration. She cites the company WD40 as an example: "If WD40 can find profound meaning in their organization, any organization can." By connecting employees to the purpose behind their work, leaders can foster engagement and loyalty.

Music as a Foundation for Leadership

Music has been a lifelong companion for Johnson, shaping her leadership philosophy. From teaching Suzuki violin lessons to co-directing the Suzuki Music Program of Los Angeles, she draws parallels between orchestral harmony and workplace collaboration.

"Collaboration goes beyond inclusion," she notes. "It means being invited to help plan and execute the vision."

Her musical background also informs her approach to resilience. She recalls guiding a longstanding member of a musical organization into an emeritus role—a delicate process that required persistence and emotional intelligence. "Creative persistence is really core to resilience and finding solutions to what appear to be insurmountable problems," Johnson says.

Storytelling, Emotional Intelligence, and Leadership

Whether on stage or in the boardroom, Johnson uses storytelling to connect with audiences emotionally.

Drawing from movies like *A Wonderful Life* and *A Christmas Carol*, she illustrates how purpose, ethics, and humanity intersect with business decisions. "The common welfare merits a valid place on the agendas of successful CEOs, CFOs, and profitable companies," she emphasizes. Positive leadership is not just ethical—it also drives measurable ROI in organizational performance.

Looking Ahead

Robin Litster Johnson continues to inspire leaders worldwide, advocating for humane, ethical, and resilient workplace cultures. Her work demonstrates that organizational success is not just about systems or numbers—it is about people, meaning, and collaboration. Her unique combination of business acumen, positive psychology, and musical artistry offers a roadmap for organizations and women leaders to thrive in the modern workplace.

Stephanie J. Bond

Breaking the Chains of Financial Abuse

Financial abuse remains one of the least understood forms of control in personal relationships, yet its impact can be deeply damaging. Stephanie J. Bond, CPA and survivor, knows this intimately. Her story sheds light on how financial control can quietly erode independence, confidence, and professional success.

What Is Financial Abuse?

Financial abuse occurs when one partner uses money or economic resources to dominate another, stripping them of independence.

It can take many forms:

- Controlling all finances and forbidding independent decisions.
- Denying access to bank accounts, credit cards, or financial documents.
- Sabotaging a partner's employment or career opportunities.
- Monitoring spending or refusing funds for basic needs.
- Stealing money or using credit without permission.

The result is often a growing dependency that traps victims alongside emotional or physical abuse, making it incredibly difficult to leave the relationship.

From Partnership to Control

Bond recounts how her marriage began as a true partnership. Together with her husband, she navigated banking, legal, and real estate ventures, sharing transparency and goals. But after she became a stay-at-home mother and managed their growing real estate business, dynamics shifted imperceptibly.

Despite outward signs of wealth—luxury cars, a beautiful home, and private school for their children—she lived on a restricted biweekly allowance for basic family needs.

Extra expenses were required to be approved, and her access to finances became limited.

Over time, her name was gradually removed from legal and financial documents, and after her husband's death, she discovered accounts had been depleted and she had no ownership rights to properties she had helped build.

Career Sabotage and Emotional Abuse

Financial abuse extended beyond money. Whenever Bond's career gained momentum, her husband would create crises or demand attention, preventing professional growth. This subtle sabotage eroded her confidence, despite her education and credentials. She recalls often feeling devalued and questioning her abilities as a result of years of control and belittlement.

Reclaiming Independence and Power

After years of navigating these challenges, Bond was able to rebuild her life. Relocating to Texas, she advanced through multiple roles, ultimately becoming CFO of a real estate company with a considerable salary. Her story illustrates how resilience, resourcefulness, and adaptability, skills developed through surviving abuse, can potentially lead to empowerment and professional success.

Lessons Learned

Bond emphasizes that financial abuse typically does not happen overnight. Small, incremental actions often compound over time, gradually stripping autonomy. Key takeaways for recognizing and preventing financial abuse include:

- Significant disparities in spending power between partners could be warning signs.
- Transparency is crucial, but conversation alone may not stop a determined abuser.

- Financial literacy and independence are important tools for self-protection.
- Emotional and financial abuses can often precede physical abuse.

A Message to Survivors

For those recognizing their own experiences in Bond's story, she offers hope: the skills developed to survive a toxic environment resilience, resourcefulness, and adaptability, can be used to reclaim a life of freedom and safety. She encourages survivors to embrace their power, pursue independence, and envision a future entirely their own.

Stephanie J. Bond's experience underscores the importance of understanding financial abuse, recognizing the warning signs, and taking steps toward autonomy and empowerment. Her story is a reminder that even after profound adversity, rebuilding a life of confidence, independence, and achievement is possible, though it may require time, effort, and support.

Tasch Turner

Storytelling, Psychology, and Building Brands That Truly Connect

In an industry saturated with algorithms, analytics, and ever-changing digital trends, Tasch Turner stands out for championing something refreshingly human: empathy. As the co-founder of Turner & Co., a boutique branding and copywriting agency, Turner has built her reputation on fusing psychology with storytelling to help brands discover—and broadcast—their most authentic voices.

"I don't buy into the whole 'success' label," Turner says. "I'm four degrees deep, run a multi-figure business, and still feel like I've only scratched the surface. The best leaders are always learning." That sentiment perfectly captures Turner's approach: ambitious yet grounded, strategic yet deeply human.

Storytelling That Starts with Listening

Ask Turner how she helps brands stand out in crowded markets, and she doesn't begin with tactics, hashtags, or trending sounds. She begins with empathy.

"Most brands are so busy shouting about themselves that they forget to listen," she explains. "At Turner & Co., we use WordCraft, a psychology-driven system that gets to the guts of what your audience actually cares about."

The process is meticulous. Turner and her team analyze a brand's DNA, vision, and values, creating what she calls a "brand bible" to align internal teams. Then they turn the lens outward, studying the target audience with almost clinical precision: What keeps them up at night? What unmet needs drive their decisions? What emotional truths do they long for a brand to acknowledge?

"That's the gold," Turner says. "From there, it's storytelling with strategy—every word anchored in data, every message designed to build real connection, not just clicks."

Breaking Barriers for Women in Business

Turner also acknowledges the unique hurdles women face in leadership roles, particularly in marketing and communications. She doesn't mince words about the competitive culture that often pits women against each other.

"You know that unspoken rule where only one woman gets a seat at the table? Rubbish," she says. "I'm here to burn that table and build a longer one."

Her advice to aspiring female leaders is direct: "Celebrate the hell out of the women around you. Champion their brilliance. And stop waiting for a roadmap—forge your own and invite others along for the ride."

It's an attitude that reflects her larger philosophy of leadership: success is not a finite pie, and lifting others only strengthens the collective.

Psychology as the Secret Weapon

One of Turner's biggest differentiators is her ability to integrate psychological insights into branding and copywriting. She recalls a client who was "stuck in the aesthetic echo chamber," posting daily content that looked polished but lacked resonance. Despite all the effort, engagement flatlined.

"Their brand was bold, cheeky, full of spark—but their content was beige, safe, blending in," she recalls.

Using her WordCraft system, Turner restructured the client's messaging around buyer psychology instead of vanity metrics.

She employed frameworks like Jobs-to-be-Done, emotional motivator mapping, and sensory language to align messaging with what audiences actually needed to hear.

"The result? Their audience started paying attention. Engagement climbed. Their voice sharpened. Best of all, they became top-of-mind in their category," Turner says. "Buyer psychology isn't just about conversions—it's about connection."

Where Creativity Meets Data

Balancing artistry with commercial strategy can be a challenge, but Turner insists the two are inseparable.

"As a creative, the toughest (and best) lesson I've learnt is this: take the ego out of your copy and let the people tell you what works," she says. "It's not about being the cleverest voice in the room, it's about being the clearest, the most useful, the most felt."

At Turner & Co., no idea is left untested. The team runs A/B/C testing, analyzes click-through rates, and tracks conversion paths to ensure creative work drives tangible results.

"Pretty doesn't pay the bills, performance does," Turner adds. "Creativity gives us the spark, but strategy gives it legs."

The Future of Storytelling in a Digital Age

As digital media continues to evolve—especially in an era increasingly shaped by artificial intelligence—Turner believes storytelling is more crucial than ever.

"For all the tech, trends, and tools that have changed, one truth hasn't: humans connect through stories," she says.

But she also warns of the risks posed by AI-generated content. While machine learning can churn out words at lightning speed, Turner believes consumers are more discerning than marketers give them credit for.

"AI copy doesn't pass the sniff test, and audiences know it," she cautions. "You can't fake connection. You can't automate authenticity."

For Turner, the future of branding lies in personal and organizational storytelling that reflects real values and resonates with genuine human emotions. "Your story is the glue," she says. "It's what builds loyalty, drives action, and creates a brand people remember."

Building Brands People Remember

Whether she's dissecting audience psychology, advising women in leadership, or blending creative artistry with rigorous testing, Tasch Turner's perspective is clear: the most successful brands are the ones that remember they're speaking to people, not profiles.

"Storytelling isn't fluff," she concludes. "It's your sharpest tool in a world full of noise. And when done right? It cuts through like nothing else."

Tina O'Banion

For many women entrepreneurs, the hardest part of running a business isn't the long hours, the competition, or even the risk: it's facing the numbers. That uncomfortable moment when profit margins, budgets, and spreadsheets start to feel like a foreign language can trigger fear and avoidance. But for **Tina O'Banion, MBA, Founder and CEO of TFO Clarity**, those very numbers became her path to empowerment.

A former Chief Financial Officer (CFO) turned author, mentor, and advocate for financial literacy, O'Banion has built a career helping leaders turn "financial fog" into crystal-clear strategy. Her acclaimed best-selling book, *Falling Up With Grace*, and her latest releases, *The C.L.A.R.I.T.Y. CODE™ Book and Workbook*, are inspiring entrepreneurs worldwide to transform their relationship with money and with themselves.

"Writing *Falling Up With Grace* and *The C.L.A.R.I.T.Y. CODE™* was both a healing process and a calling," O'Banion shares. "I kept journals during my years as a senior finance executive—notes about the challenges, missteps, and lessons I experienced leading through financial chaos.

When I started working with entrepreneurs through my own firm, I saw those same struggles repeat themselves, just in smaller businesses with higher stakes."

It was then that O'Banion realized a truth that would define her mission: entrepreneurs aren't failing because they lack drive or talent, they're struggling because they're trying to lead without clarity.

Turning Confusion into Confidence

Through her firm **TFO Clarity**, O'Banion and her team deliver accounting and fractional CFO services that bridge the gap between accounting and strategy. Her seven-step framework, **The C.L.A.R.I.T.Y. CODE™**, distills decades of financial expertise into a practical roadmap for entrepreneurs to regain control of their numbers and their narrative.

"The 'C' in the C.L.A.R.I.T.Y. Code stands for 'Calculate,'" she explains. "You can't grow what you don't measure. Too many business owners rely solely on bookkeepers to pay bills and CPAs to file taxes but neither role is designed to help you truly understand how your business is performing."

It's a common blind spot that O'Banion has witnessed countless times.

A company may look successful on paper, hitting seven figures in revenue, yet still run out of cash because the owner doesn't grasp their margins or burn rate. "By the time they realize the problem, it's too late," she warns. "Clarity isn't just about cash flow; it's about understanding how every number connects to the bigger picture."

From CFO to Author: The Power of Storytelling

Rather than write another technical finance manual, O'Banion chose a deeply personal approach. Her protagonist, **Grace**, is an entrepreneur inspired by her grandmother—a resilient woman who faced hardship with determination.

"Through Grace, I wanted readers to see themselves," O'Banion says. "The mistakes, the resilience, the growth, all of it. Not every entrepreneur survives their financial missteps, but Grace does, and she learns that financial clarity is her turning point."

The emotional honesty behind *Falling Up With Grace* struck a chord with readers, especially women business owners balancing ambition, self-doubt, and societal expectations. For many, it wasn't just a book, it was a mirror.

"Falling down is part of the process," O'Banion writes. "But when you lead with clarity, you fall up."

Mindset Over Math: Redefining Leadership Through Finance

If there's one lesson O'Banion wants every business leader to embrace, it's that **budgeting is not a task, it's a leadership discipline**.

"Most owners treat budgeting as a once-a-year exercise," she explains. "But a real budget is a living strategy. It reflects your priorities, your goals, and your ability to adapt."

That perspective transforms finance from a reactive activity into a proactive growth engine. At TFO Clarity, O'Banion helps entrepreneurs build budgets that drive decisions, not just document them. She encourages leaders to review their finances monthly, not just annually to make smarter, faster, and more confident choices.

"When every dollar has a job, and every metric has meaning," she says, "your budget becomes more than a plan, it becomes your growth engine."

Leading Through Uncertainty

O'Banion's years as a CFO taught her that true leadership during financial challenges depends on two factors: **transparency and tempo**.

"Transparency builds trust," she says. "When your team knows you're aware of the challenges and working through them, they stay engaged. Silence only creates fear."

Tempo, on the other hand, is about rhythm and creating structure amid uncertainty. That's where her concept of **'Money Monday'** was born: a weekly check-in for leaders to review numbers, assess changes, and stay grounded.

She also developed a **progress journal**, designed to help leaders reflect and recalibrate every week across all areas of their business.

"Great leaders don't need to have all the answers," she emphasizes. "They just need to be brave enough to ask the right questions and ask them consistently."

Rewriting the Story Around Numbers

For many entrepreneurs, fear of finance stems from an old, limiting story: "I'm not a numbers person." O'Banion challenges that belief head-on.

"Most people who avoid the numbers aren't irresponsible, they're afraid," she says. "Somewhere along the way, they were told they weren't good at math, and that stuck. But numbers aren't judgment, they're information. Once you learn to read them, you unlock the power to lead."

That mindset shift is at the heart of *The C.L.A.R.I.T.Y. CODE*™, a story-driven framework built to make financial mastery accessible. The accompanying workbook and masterclass offer step-by-step tools for CEOs to implement seven proven strategies that top-performing businesses use every day.

"Financial clarity isn't optional," O'Banion says firmly. "It's the foundation for leading like a CFO and growing like a CEO."

Tina O'Banion's message is clear, courageous, and timely. As more women step into leadership and entrepreneurship, her work reminds us that clarity, financial and emotional power is not just power, but peace.

"The numbers don't define you," she says. "They guide you. And once you learn to trust them, you'll never fear them again."

Financial clarity isn't optional—it's the foundation for leading like a CFO and growing like a CEO.

Veronique Gautier

Leading from Alignment

For many women who have spent decades building careers, raising families, and meeting the expectations of others in life and business, a quiet but persistent question often arises: *Is this all there is?* Beneath the achievements and responsibilities, a quiet longing can emerge—to live more authentically: to reconnect with purpose, find meaning, and redefine life from within.

That's where transformation strategist and leadership mentor Veronique Gautier, known to her clients simply as V, steps in.

A seasoned entrepreneur and visionary guide, V works with high-performing women navigating major life transitions—from post-career reinvention to burnout recovery to post-divorce recalibration.

Her mission is not about superficial change; it's about creating a life that better aligns with who her clients truly are now—not who they were once expected to be.

When the Old Life No Longer Fits

"These women aren't lost—they just haven't evolved the way they see themselves, which makes it difficult to evolve how they express themselves," V says. "They're stuck in an outdated identity. They come to me when the life they built no longer feels quite right."

Her clients are often feeling exhausted, stuck in roles that no longer resonate with them, or simply searching for a deeper sense of fulfillment. What they seek isn't just a pivot—it's a meaningful shift. V offers a comprehensive, science-informed approach to transformation, blending strategy, neuroscience, and personal growth practices.

The Four Questions that May Change Everything

At the heart of V's methodology is a simple yet impactful framework: The Four Questions to Reinvention. This process invites women to reflect on who they are now, what they genuinely want, and how to express that authentically in the world.

Who am I now? This first question helps shed external labels and outdated identities. Through her signature Distinctive Natural Assets® process, V guides clients to reconnect with their deep authentic selves and uncover their unique source of value.

What do I want now? Using visioning techniques inspired by DreamBuilder® principles, clients begin to imagine a life they genuinely desire—and start moving toward it. "When you think from the dream, you begin to create it," V notes.

As clients begin taking action based on their vision—rather than their current circumstances or limitations—the noise and distractions fade, and a clearer path begins to take shape. This is what V calls Spiritual DNA®. Along the way, they discover their Distinctive Natural Influence: the unique impact they are naturally inclined to create through their innate gifts. This accelerates their growth and alignment exponentially, fast-forwarding their evolution.

This final stage transforms clarity of personal identity into outward expression. Through her Business DNA® model, V helps clients uncover how they're uniquely equipped to lead, contribute, and innovate.

From this foundation, they build a distinct vehicle for their expression and impact—at minimum, a personal brand, and for many, a vision-led business or purpose-driven venture.

More Than Mindset: A Systemic Reboot

"This isn't just mindset work," V explains. "We go straight to the core—reboot the nervous system, unkink the subconscious hose, and repattern emotional habits to support new decision-making and actions."

Her work draws from neuroplasticity, epigenetics, quantum field theory, and psychology to foster rapid and sustainable transformation.

Clients often report a sense of renewed vitality, improved focus, and a deeper sense of peace. "True well-being is alignment," V says. "When your thoughts, feelings, and actions are congruent, you come alive."

A Journey Rooted in Experience

V's work is grounded in her own story of reinvention. Once a very successful corporate strategist in NYC, she found herself overwhelmed as a new mother, struggling to balance family, health, and identity. "I lost myself trying to meet everyone else's needs," she recalls. "And then everything unraveled."

From that crisis emerged a deeper calling. V immersed herself in neuroscience, quantum physics application, and human development, eventually creating a transformational methodology that blends evidence-based tools with intuitive insight. Today, she shares this system through private mentorship and programs available at veronique-gautier.com.

Where Inner Clarity Meets Innovation: The branDNAlab

For those ready to express their vision into the world, V offers the possibility to partner with The BrandnaLab, an innovation studio dedicated to supporting vision-led leadership expression.

Through her Business DNA® framework, V helps clients build personal brands, transform businesses and organizations, or develop innovative thought leadership platforms that reflect their deep authentic selves and unique vision.

"I believe everyone is unique and it is by design," she says. "Each of us carries a unique design (DNA) and it's up to us to express it as powerfully as we can.

It takes knowing who you are and owning it through everything you are and do. Life-to-business. That is why we start with the Founder. Once that's clear, the rest becomes clearer."

Whether launching a new venture or evolving an existing business, The BrandnaLab supports leaders in shaping purpose-driven work that is both meaningful and sustainable. With her team, V personally focuses on initiatives with significant societal impact—what she calls "Tech for Humans." Learn more at thebrandnalab.com.

Redefining Success Through Vitality

In a performance-driven world, V challenges the traditional metrics of success. For her, the new gold standard is what she calls 'full-life vitality.'

"Too many high-achieving women are running on adrenaline," she says. "But burnout isn't a badge—it's a sign that things are out of alignment." Her approach teaches clients to source energy from coherence—where what we think, how we feel, and what we do are fully aligned.

"When you're in integrity with yourself, vitality returns. Not because you're chasing it—but because you've stopped resisting who you are."

A New Vision, A New Chapter

Ultimately, V's work is about more than reinvention. It's about vision-led leadership—helping women not just "figure things out," but become who they're designed to be and express that identity powerfully in the world.

"This is the future of Act 2," she says. "It's not about proving anything. It's about showing up as your truest self. When you do that, you don't just walk into a room—you shift it."

Standing at the Edge of What's Next?

For women ready to begin again—with clarity, confidence, and vitality—V offers more than strategies. She offers a system for reclaiming the full expression of who you are.

"This work begins the moment you choose yourself," she says. "Not someday. Now."

Linda Fisk

Advancing Women's Leadership & Empowerment

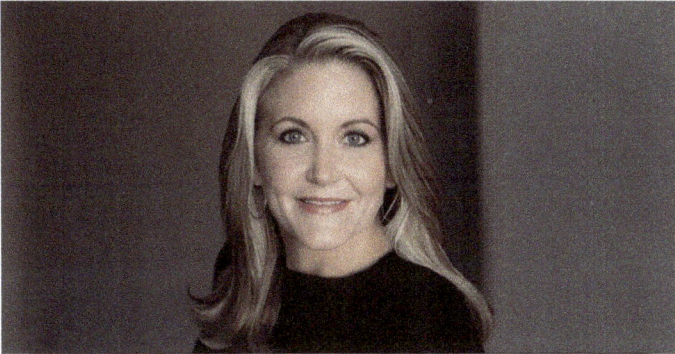

I had always been told that I was special. My parents desperately wanted to have a child, and I was told that of all the children they could have chosen, they adopted me. That made me unique, chosen and special. And, I was told that it was good to be different; that being different made you more memorable. And, there was no way to hide that I was different…That I was certainly adopted, rather than born, into this family. You see, my Father was American Indian, and my Mother was Asian – and I was a blonde, blue-eyed, little girl with alabaster skin. So, I didn't look like either of my parents, or our extended families. But my parents always reassured me that being distinctive makes you more interesting; and being different makes you surprising. And, that's good.

As a family, we were often described as unusual, different or strange. In any public outing, I would catch the inquisitive glances, and even accusatory stares, as people tried to fit the puzzle pieces together. Sometimes, we would catch the whispers of those around us, asking about who the little girl really belonged to.

Sometimes, the well-meaning stranger would be bold enough to directly ask my parents, "Who are you babysitting for?" or "Who does the little girl belong to?" And, without hesitation, my parents would announce, "She is our daughter" without the need for further explanation.

But, my parents would reassure me that it takes courage to grow up and turn out to be who you really are. My parents didn't want me to adopt their culture, their physical attributes, their characteristics, or even their personality. They simply encouraged me to discover who I was and to embrace my differences, because those points of differentiation will become my story. That will lead to uncovering my unique genius.

Over the years, I've learned that your differences, what other people may consider to be your flaws, hold the key to what makes you incredibly special - and your unique genius. Sometimes, being flawed, and being very open and transparent about it, can be the most attractive trait of all. In fact, most people want to follow leaders that are brilliant, despite being human and having flaws.

It's very common for leaders to feel the pressure to assimilate, to acquiesce, to homogenize. As we look to what other successful leaders are doing, what they are saying, what they are recommending, it's natural to emulate them. In fact, this practice has been institutionalized in the process of benchmarking.

We try to find out what other are doing right and then we do the same thing. We minimize our differences, and we try to replicate the practices of other successful leaders.

But, when everyone in an industry starts copying the leaders, over time, the entire industry starts to look the same, feel the same, and sound the same. There are no differences. Nothing distinguishes one leader from another. As Youngme Moon explains in *Different – Escaping the Competitive Herd*, "The dynamic is not unlike a popularity contest in which everyone tries to win by being equal parts friendly, happy, active and fun. Or an election campaign in which all the candidates try to charming, serious, humble and strong. Once everyone starts doing it, no one stands out." It's a downward spiral of conformity, in a sea of sameness.

And, the best leaders often emphasize their perceived flaws, they admit their mistakes and shortcomings, and openly talk about how they have learned from their failures. These leaders focus on the learning, the strength, the resilience and the growth they have experienced through flaws, mistakes, failures, missteps and shortcomings.

They accent them, feature them, highlight them, expose them, call attention to them, and openly display them. Their uniqueness is a signature part of who they are. They purposefully admit to their points of difference and they embrace their perceived flaws as a way of highlighting their own unique learning journey which has cultivated their genius.

But, how do you begin to identify those aspects of your story, your identity, your leadership that makes you distinctive and different? How do you find your genius?

Make a list of every possible limitation you can think of that prevents you from being the leader that you think everyone expects. Include information about your own fears and doubts, as well as any perceived shortage of opportunities to be a leader that everyone respects and admires. Then examine each one carefully and decide if it's really true or not. You may be surprised at some of the things you've convinced yourself to believe!

Indeed, failure and flaws are often why successful people achieve such remarkable heights of greatness: They learn from their setbacks, failures and mistakes, and then get back up and apply these learnings to their next attempt. Some of the most successful people have encountered disappointing setbacks based on perceived flaws:

Walt Disney was fired from a newspaper and was told he "lacked imagination and had no good ideas."

Oprah Winfrey was fired early in her career as a TV reporter because she was told she was "unfit for TV."

Dr. Seuss had his first book rejected by 27 different publishers.

Bill Gates was a Harvard dropout and started a failed first business called Traf-O-Data.

When we approach our own failures, flaws and differences with a spirit of generosity, we counteract the sensation of being under attack, being judged harshly. The key is to turn the focus away from ourselves — away from whether our flaws and our failures will be judged harshly by others — and toward helping those around us accept their own points of difference.

Showing kindness and generosity to others, and helping others see their unique attributes and characteristics, has been shown to engender courage, acceptance and confidence.

Ironically, it's being imperfect that makes us real and relatable. We often connect with others over our insecurities, quirks, and struggles. People who are truly interested in you and care about you, don't expect you to be perfect; they want you to be authentic. Embracing your imperfections and letting others see the less than perfect parts of you, allows you to connect more deeply—to love others and be loved fully.

Choose connection over perfection.

You don't have to prove your worth. You don't have to please everyone all the time. You don't have to compare yourself to others. You don't have to measure up to anyone else's idea of beauty, success, or worthiness. Some people will like you—and some won't. And that's OK.

What you'll gain is freedom. Freedom to be yourself, to do what feels right for you, to pursue your interests, to follow your values, to wear whatever you want, to explore who you are. Nobody's perfect, but we all have value—and we don't have to keep trying to prove it.

Choose to let others see your real self rather than hiding behind a facade of perfection. Genius isn't about being perfect. In fact, genius is seeing the world in a completely new way.

Your differences make you surprising, and memorable.

We remember the unusual events in our lives, not the common ones. When we experience something different, we want to tell other people about it. Surprising experiences are remembered, and shared with others.

And, we remember the people in our lives that are unique, distinctive. If you are remarkable enough, someone might even write a social media post, a blog, or a book about you. Fitting in and following the lead of others simply makes us invisible. If we fit in, we don't get any attention. And, attention is one of the most valuable gifts we can receive.

There are no good substitutes for you, in all your uniqueness.

Being unique is about being different, being unusual and being uncommon. Unfortunately, instead of embracing our uniqueness, we often try to hide it in an effort to be more normal. We tend to focus on the ways we are similar to others, not different. Because of this bias, its helpful to spend some time thinking about what makes you odd, atypical, and exceptional. But, don't focus on trying to fix your perceived weaknesses, flaws or differences. Appreciate them by discovering that your weaknesses are important clues to your most powerful strengths.

Our uniqueness can be a part of our superpower and it can reveal our genius.

Consider that Barbara Corcoran, TV personality on Shark Tank, successful entrepreneur and investor, keynote speaker, best-selling author, and owner of real estate brokerage firm The Corcoran Group, was labeled as "the dumb kid" that couldn't read or write, due to dyslexia. Barbara's credits include straight D's in high school and college and 20 jobs by the time she turned 23. But, the Corcoran Group is now the largest and best-known brand in the brokerage business, building the largest and best-known brand in the business.

How did a dyslexic woman, who couldn't read or write, build such a successful business? You could argue that Barbara succeeded because of her flaws, not in spite of them. Because of her weaknesses, she had to trust others and rely on them to help her run the business. This evolved into a culture of cooperation, collaboration and teamwork, rather than fierce competition, which separated The Corcoran Group from their competitors. Barbara hired people who were strong where she was weak.

Barbara's intuitive intelligence and racing mind made her impatient and easily frustrated, creating a sense of urgency that motivated people to make changes and improvements. Because Barbara was restless, she spent most of her time out of her office, working with clients, looking for properties, observing the market. Because Barbara was impulsive, she quickly implemented innovative new ideas that differentiated her brokerage firm.

Barbara didn't just appreciate her own weaknesses, she also created an organization that appreciated the differences of others.

This created a culture of innovation, trust and teamwork that truly separates The Corcoran Group from any other brokerage in New York. And, that became Barbara Corcoran's genius.

Appreciate, rather than adjust and adapt.

Conventional wisdom suggests that you should build on your strengths and fix weaknesses. Don't appreciate your flaws. Instead, adjust and adapt. But, every weakness has a corresponding strength that leads to your unique genius. Appreciate that your flaws, because that is what makes you awesome.

We need to find ways to capitalize on our unique characteristics and use our apparent flaws to our advantage. Striving for all-around excellence leads directly to mediocrity. As we try to fix our weaknesses, we often end up damaging our corresponding strengths.

Decide what trade-offs you will make – where you will do things badly, even very badly, in the service of being great at what makes you different, what makes your unique and reveals your genius. Reframe criticism you receive as a sign that you're doing something right.

Assess and then amplify your differences.

What are your unique weaknesses? Differences? Flaws? Now what would happen if you actually maximized them? Openly admitting your limitations helps us build trust. This is true when discussing our own limitations, or those of our ideas, products or services.

Admitting weaknesses can make your core ideas more powerful, and allow you to be more influential.

Amplifying your differences is about spending more time, energy and resources on what makes us unique. And, effective leadership is not about changing people. It's about accepting and respecting who they are, and finding ways to help them succeed. Great leaders help people become more of who they are. Instead of forcing people to fit in, we need to help them find the right fit. And they help cultivate and nurture the genius of others.

Be proud of who you are and what you represent. Take full ownership of your strengths, as well as your weaknesses. Don't apologize for your flaws, and don't try to fix them. Instead, exploit and amplify your imperfections, and embrace your differences. There are an infinite number of ways to be unique. Remember, the most impactful, memorable and successful leaders are considered mavericks. They are different. They are unusual.

It is good to be flawed – in fact it is inevitable. Embrace your uniqueness. Exploit your differences. Confound expectations. Being different makes you rare. Being normal makes you ordinary.

So, what's different about you?

LeadHERship®
GLOBAL

Our Mission

We are the only organization embracing the passion of high-performing women to positively impact their lives and accelerate their success by integrating self-directed learning, impactful group experiences, and expert-led coaching and mentoring.

Authentic Relationships

Cultivate Authentic Relationships

Build enduring relationships. Compassionately support and challenge each other — in service of accelerating our collective success.

Rise together.

Courage

Act With Courage

Faithfully pursue long-term purpose and impact. Support individual freedom and integrity. Serve our mission with integrity.

Lean in.

Commitment

Dedicate Yourself

Demonstrate passion and commitment. Take ownership of your thoughts, words, and actions. Be consistent and deliver results.

Create value.

Growth

Be a Lifetime Learner

Maintain a sense of curious inquiry. Recognize that we are all on a learning journey. Seek to understand and support one another.

Deepen congruence.

Community

Celebrate Each Other

Share, learn, and grow in a trusting community. Lift each other up, encourage and celebrate one another. Share stories and create memories.

Spread the love.

The LeadHERShip Advantage

We harness the knowledge, influence, and trust of high-performing women to stimulate idea exchange, support creativity, provide access to critical resources and tools, and accelerate both personal and professional growth.

https://leadhershipglobal.com